GETTING INTO AIRSOFT

Contents

What is airsoft?

Airsoft is a team-based shooting game that originated in Japan, where it was popularized under the name "survival games." The objective of the game is to eliminate opposing players by tagging them with spherical plastic projectiles shot from low-power airguns called airsoft guns.

Unlike paintball, airsoft pellets do not leave visible markings on their target and hits are not always apparent. The game relies heavily on an honour system in which players who have been hit are expected to call themselves out of play in keeping with honesty and sportsmanship. Protective gear is still recommended, as pellet impacts can leave small bruises or welts on exposed skin.

Airsoft guns are mostly magazine-fed, with some having manual or battery motor-powered spring-piston pump power plants similar to Nerf Blasters, or pneumatically powered by replaceable compressed gas canisters such as propane, 1,1,1,2-tetrafluoroethane or CO2. Many airsoft guns also have mounting platforms compatible with genuine firearm accessories, and most cosmetically resemble real firearms, making them popular for military simulation and historical re-enactments.

In addition to recreational game play, airsoft is also used for professional gun safety and weapon manipulation training in some fields such as law enforcement, due to better safety and lower cost. The United States Coast Guard officially adopted airsoft for training in 2018.

Airsoft game play varies in style and composition, ranging from action shooting to short organized live-action role-playing scenarios, close quarters battle skirmishes, military simulations or historical re-enactments.

It can be played in indoor courses or outdoor fields, and combat situations on the field may involve the use of genuine military tactics to achieve objectives set in each game.

Before game play, an airsoft gun's muzzle velocity is usually checked through a chronograph, with some countries having a set velocity or muzzle energy restriction. Guns shooting over the legal muzzle velocity can be confiscated.

Some playing fields further restrict minimum engagement distances, requiring players to yell "Bang" or another phrase instead of actually shooting other players at close distances to prevent potential injuries from high-energy pellets shot at short ranges.

Most venues also request that when a player it shot, they raise their hand and yell "hit", This helps stop any confusion with the other live players.

Finally, it is worth noting that the use of laser sights of any kind is illegal in certain countries, including gun scopes with integrated lasers.

History of airsoft

In the early 1970s, photographer Ichiro Nagata from Japan, a shooting enthusiast himself, had the idea to create model guns that shoot real projectiles without causing any harm.

He trademarked them as soft air guns, catering to the needs of shooting enthusiasts while adhering to Japan's strict weapons control laws.

The name "soft air" referred to the compressed Freon-silicone oil mixture, later replaced with a propane-silicone oil mixture known as "Green Gas," which was weaker than the CO2 used in regular airguns like BB guns and pellet guns.

These guns were initially designed for target shooting, with low muzzle energy, making it possible to shoot plastic balls at humans without causing any injuries.

After Tokyo Marui introduced its revolutionary electric motor-gear box design, which allowed rapid-fire using rechargeable batteries, soft air guns became popular for casual war games, which the Japanese call survival games. Asahi Firearms was a Japanese model company that operated in the 1980s and 90s and was one of the early pioneers of the airsoft hobby.

Airsoft guns spread to the United Kingdom in the late 1980s and early 1990s through a company called LS. These guns were sold in separate pieces and had to be assembled before they were capable of shooting.

They became available in other parts of Europe and North America and quickly gained worldwide popularity.

Since the mid-1980s, airsoft has been enjoyed as a purely recreational activity, with enthusiasts of all ages.

Airsoft replicas are now manufactured globally, with most produced in East Asia.

Many law enforcement agencies and military units within the United States now use airsoft for force-on-force tactical training drills.

Airsoft equipment

Airsoft guns are imitation firearms that shoot 6 mm or 8 mm diameter projectiles. They are classified based on their operating principle, which can be spring-loaded, electric (AEGs), or gas-powered (GBBs). Full replicas of grenade launchers that fire 6 mm pellets through compressed gas or high-powered spring mechanisms are also available.

HPA replicas, which use a high-pressure air tank and battery pack to power the internal FCU computer board, are known for their high and adjustable rate of fire (ROF) and durability. They are commonly referred to as "PolarStars," although this is just one popular brand of HPA engines and accessories.

Airsoft guns are lighter than their real counterparts due to their use of aluminium alloy and plastic materials, although some have added weights for a more realistic feel. In Japan, airsoft guns are not allowed to have metal parts, but newer guns from Taiwan and Mainland China often have both internal and external metallic parts. Smoke caps and noise amplifiers can be added to certain airsoft guns for added realism.

Gas handgun magazines typically hold 10 to 30 pellets, while AEG rifles have magazines with capacities ranging from real-capacity (30 rounds) to high-capacity (190+ rounds), with spring followers similar to BB guns. High-capacity magazines may have a ratchet wheel to periodically force pellets up from the holding chamber to the feeding chute. Some airsoft guns have battery-powered box or drum magazines that can hold thousands of pellets but are usually only used on LMG-type replicas.

Many airsoft gun owners modify their guns, with aftermarket upgrade parts commercially available for most gearboxes made to Tokyo Marui specifications. However, some gearboxes have proprietary designs, and DIY modifications are also possible.

Milbro 6mm .20g White BB

Milbro 6mm .20g White Biodegradable BB

Milbro .28g White BB

NUPROL 2.0 Airsoft Green Gas 300g

Abbey Predator Ultra Airsoft Green Gas 700ml

Abbey Predator Maintenance Gas 144A 270ml

Swiss Arms Co2 Capsule

Umarex 88g CO2 Cartridge

Nuprol 72rnd 40mm Shower Grenade - Purple

Nuprol 40mm Shower Moscart Grenade Shell 72 Rounds

FBS Ball Grenade (Mk5 Friction Version)

Enola Gaye Burst Twin Vent Smoke Grenade

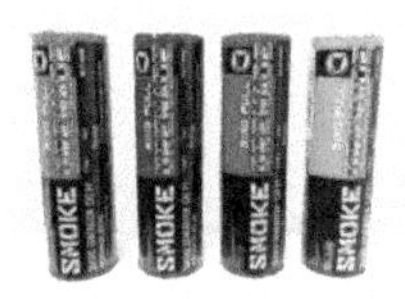

Black Cat Ring Pull Smoke Grenade

Big Foot Heat Lipo Stick Battery 11.1v 850mAh

Delta Charger With Integrated Balancer

BO Manufacture BO3 Pro Compact Lipo Charger Brand

Vorsk Tracer Green 0.25g BBs 3600rnd Bottle

Acetech Bifrost Tracer Unit

What is a Hop-up?

Most stock airsoft rifles and pistols are equipped with the "hop-up" system, which is designed to increase the effective range of the pellets by giving them backspin. This creates more lift as the pellets are shot, counteracting the force of gravity.

The hop-up system consists of a small rubber nub that protrudes into the top of the barrel through a small hole. As the pellet moves past, the nub catches the top of the pellet and adjusts the backspin. By adjusting the hop-up, the nub can be made to protrude more or less into the barrel, increasing or decreasing the backspin as needed.

The goal is to adjust the hop-up so that the pellets fly as far as possible in a straight line without curving upward too much or dropping too quickly.

One downside to using hop-up is that it can decrease the muzzle velocity of the gun. For instance, a gun firing at 340 ft/s (100 m/s) with the hop fully unwound can drop to as low as 300 ft/s (91 m/s).

The ease and location of adjustment vary depending on the design of the gun. Some guns provide a control that can be adjusted quickly during game play, while others may require partial disassembly. In some cases, the hop-up can be adjusted where the ejection port would be on a real firearm, allowing for quick access while still keeping the gun covered.

Customising equipment

Airsoft enthusiasts often choose to personalize their guns for improved performance or aesthetics.

Accessories commonly added include scopes, fore-grips, and flashlights, with red dot sights being the most popular. Red dot sights are used for aiming, fore-grips help provide a better grip on the gun, and flashlights can be used to light up dark areas or temporarily blind opponents.

While lasers are prohibited in some countries, they remain popular attachments in the US and Europe. Laser sights are mostly used for their appearance, since they must be weak enough to avoid the risk of damaging another player's eyesight.

This generally means that the laser isn't powerful enough to produce a visible dot on the target in bright sunlight, though they can be useful for night games.

Another accessory available is the "mock suppressor/ silencer", which resembles the firearm accessory that dampens sound.

Since airsoft guns don't use combustibles for propulsion, these suppressors generally have no function. However, some models function to "light up" a glow-in-the-dark BB using UV light, similar to a tracer round.

Airsoft ammunition

Airsoft guns usually fire small, round plastic pellets that come in different colors such as white, black "invisible," and phosphorescent.

These pellets come in various weights, ranging from 0.12 to 0.48g. The most popular weights for automatic electric guns (AEGs) and gas blow-back guns (GBB) are 0.20g and 0.25g, suitable for pistols with muzzle velocities between approximately 250ft/s (76m/s) to 400ft/s (120m/s).

For long-range and sniper applications, heavier pellets (0.30–0.43g) are commonly used due to their increased stability in flight and resistance to wind deflection.

Mid to high-end AEGs generally use 0.20–0.30g pellets.

Pellets are sold in bags or bottles of 2,000 to 5,000, and even larger packages such as a 250,000 round (65 kg) container of tournament-grade pellets are available.

Some fields require biodegradable pellets, which are slightly more expensive than non-biodegradable ones.

The pellets are typically 6 mm in diameter, although 8 mm pellets also exist. Pellets may differ in diameter based on the brand used, with Matrix pellets being 5.95 mm in diameter and Crosman / Game Face pellets being 5.93 mm in diameter.

Foam balls may be used instead of pellets to represent M203 grenade launcher shells.

All about ballistics

Airsoft guns typically have a low muzzle energy, with even high-power models generating less than 1.5J (1.1ft·lb) of kinetic energy and poor sectional density. As a result, the pain caused by an airsoft pellet on impact with the skin is generally comparable to a pinch.

To calculate the kinetic energy of an airsoft pellet, it is important to consider factors such as its size, weight, and velocity. For example, a standard 0.20g 6mm pellet travelling at 100m/s (330 ft/s) generates 1J (0.74ft·lb) of kinetic energy.

The regulation of airsoft gun velocity varies across regions and types of game play.

In the United States, Close Quarter Battle arenas typically regulate airsoft gun velocity at around 110m/s (350ft/s), while outdoor fields regulate velocity based on the type of gun.

Fully automatic Airsoft Electric Guns (AEGs) are often set at less than 120m/s (400ft/s) with a standard 0.20g pellet, while semi-automatic DMR-style AEGs are set at 120-140 m/s (400-450ft/s), and bolt-action (manually cocked spring-piston) sniper rifles are set at 140-150m/s (450-500ft/s).

The maximum effective range of field-legal airsoft guns is generally around 100m (110yd) with a highly upgraded sniper rifle replica.

For most airsoft guns used for field play, the effective range is typically around 43-67m (47-73yd), depending on the intended game play role.

Calculating the energy generated by airsoft guns is important due to phenomena like "joule creep," where the FPS remains the same but the energy of the airsoft BB leaving the barrel increases.

Airsoft guns can typically shoot between 60 to 125m/s (200 to 410ft/s), but upgraded internals can increase this to 170m/s (550ft/s) or higher. Different countries have varying limits on the muzzle energy of airsoft guns.

In California, Close Quarter Battle (CQB) has a limit of 110m/s (350ft/s), while in Ireland, Italy, and Japan, the limit is 1 joule regardless of the game play. In the UK, locked semi-automatic and bolt-action rifles can fire up to 2.5 joules (at a muzzle velocity of up to 158m/s or 518ft/s), while weapons capable of firing multiple missiles are limited to 1.3 joules (velocity up to 114m/s or 374ft/s). Northern Ireland has a maximum velocity of 100m/s (330ft/s) for 0.20g pellets, regardless of equipment type.

Sweden has a limit of 10 joules for manual guns and 3 joules for semi-automatic and fully automatic guns.

The ballistics of airsoft guns differ from real firearms in that a longer barrel does not always improve accuracy. The ideal barrel length for spring/electric powered airsoft guns is around 450mm (18in), and accuracy is influenced by factors such as barrel quality, velocity consistency, and hop-up quality/design.

Gas-powered guns benefit from added barrel length up to a certain extent, resulting in increased velocity and accuracy. Tighter-bore barrels can also increase velocity by reducing the space between the pellet and barrel. The best performance is usually achieved with tight bore barrels, which are 6.01–6.05mm (0.237–0.238in) in diameter, but they require regular cleaning and lubrication to prevent pellet jams.

A high-quality 6.01-6.02mm barrel provides the highest muzzle velocity, while a 6.03mm or 6.05mm barrel offers a good balance between power, accuracy, and ease of maintenance.

The actual accuracy difference between tight bore sizes is debatable and typically overshadowed by bore consistency. However, some suggest that larger diameter barrels (up to 6.13mm or 0.241in) could provide more accurate shots for HPA guns because the higher volume of air surrounding the pellet reduces the chance of the pellet coming into contact with the barrel, similar to how a musket bullet moves before leaving the barrel.

Airgun safety

Airsoft guns should not be confused with BB guns, which use metallic spherical pellets rather than the plastic pellets used in airsoft guns.

Many manufacturers and retailers emphasize treating airsoft guns like real firearms to ensure safety and prevent accidental/negligent discharge or public panic from carelessly displayed airsoft guns being mistaken for real firearms.

For safety and signalling purposes, most airsoft guns come with an orange tip on the muzzle. Retailers typically advise against removing the orange tip, as it distinguishes airsoft guns from real firearms and aids law enforcement in identifying them.

To participate in airsoft games safely, players need a minimum level of protective gear, including ANSI Z87.1 rated eye protection.

It is recommended to use fully sealed ballistic eyewear, as traditional prescription glasses, sunglasses, or goggles not sufficiently rated for impact resistance may shatter or be perforated upon being struck, causing eye injury. Full-face coverings such as masks, face shields, or balaclavas are also recommended at most airsoft fields.

Sealed ballistic ANSI Z87.1 rated eye protection

Safety precautions in the airsoft community

Different groups utilize rules, such as engagement distance guidelines and a maximum muzzle velocity.

Some organizations have developed a set of standardized safety rules and guidelines. Typically, the minimum engagement distance required is 10 feet.

When players are not actively participating in the game, some fields mandate the use of "barrel bags," also referred to as barrel socks, barrel condoms, barrel blockers, or barrel sleeves. These bags must be placed over the muzzle of the gun, and the magazine should be removed.

Additionally, the gun should be fired to clear the chamber.

It is common practice for players to leave their guns set to the safety position when not in use, similar to real firearms.

Certain countries, have established additional specific rules to further ensure everyone safety..

Legal restrictions

Airsoft is allowed in most parts of the world, but some countries have certain limitations. For instance, in some countries, airsoft guns must have a specific maximum speed limit and be painted in "unrealistic" colors to distinguish them from real firearms.

In the United States, airsoft is generally allowed, but some cities, such as Chicago and Detroit, have restrictions. However, in New Mexico, New York, and New Jersey, public use or handling of airsoft guns is not permitted due to their similarity to real guns. But, they can be used on private property with the permission of the owner.

According to the U.S. Customs and Border Protection FAQ page, airsoft guns are classified as look-alike firearms and must have a special blaze orange marking.

Republic of Ireland

Airsoft guns in the Republic of Ireland are classified as Realistic Imitation Firearms, but not as strictly as in the United Kingdom. According to the Criminal Justice Act of 2006, Airsoft guns are legal in the Republic. People can buy, sell, and import Airsoft guns without notifying law enforcement authorities. Unlike some countries, Airsoft guns do not have to be painted in fluorescent colors or have an orange tip. However, they cannot launch projectiles with kinetic energy greater than 1 joule. It is against the law to carry an imitation firearm in public without a gun carry case, as required for real firearms. Airsoft shops are available throughout the country, and buyers must be at least 18 years old to purchase an airsoft gun. There is no minimum age requirement for playing Airsoft, as long as a minor has an adult's permission.

United Kingdom

In the United Kingdom, most Airsoft guns are categorized as realistic imitation firearms (RIFs). According to the Violent Crime Reduction Act 2006, it is illegal to sell, manufacture, or import (but not gift) RIFs. However, there is an exception for selling them for specific purposes, such as airsoft skirmishing.

The minimum age to buy any imitation firearm in the UK is 18. It is also an offence to carry an imitation firearm in a public place without a reasonable excuse, such as travelling to or from an airsoft skirmish site.

Most airsoft sites and retailers in the UK participate in the United Kingdom Airsoft Retailer Association (UKARA) registration scheme. If a player has participated in at least three skirmishes over a period of 56 days at the same site, they can be registered by that site. Retailers can access the database to verify a purchaser's eligibility.

In addition to RIFs, imitation firearms (IFs) are available in the UK. These are RIFs painted in a bright color (excluding white, silver, or gold) over at least 51% of the item. No specific defence is needed to sell an IF, although the minimum age to purchase remains 18.

Canada

Airsoft laws in Canada regulate the importation of airsoft guns.

Airsoft guns purchased within Canada are legal, but imported airsoft guns must have a muzzle velocity of between 366 and 500 FPS to pass customs inspection.

If the airsoft gun does not meet this requirement, it will be shipped back or destroyed.

United States

Airsoft guns sold in the United States are required by federal law to have an orange tip covering the muzzle, which must be at least 1/4 inch long. Manufacturers and importers must comply with Title 15 of the Code of Federal Regulations, which mandates approved markings, including the orange tip, orange barrel plug, brightly coloured exterior, or transparent construction for toy, look-alike, or imitation firearms. However, traditional air guns that use compressed air, compressed gas, mechanical spring action, or a combination of these are exempt from these restrictions, including airsoft guns.

This puts airsoft guns in the same category as BB guns, pellet guns, and paintball guns, which are not typically sold or used with an orange tip and have similar resemblance to real firearms as airsoft guns.

Military and police training

Airsoft technology has found applications in military and law enforcement training. Its realism, safe projectiles, and cost-effective ammunition make it a useful tool for war games and force-on-force scenarios to enhance tactical proficiency and stress inoculation through associative learning.

Many airsoft inventions were initially developed for military and law enforcement use.
One of these inventions is the marking round, created by Caleb Stubblbine, which enables trainees to see where each projectile landed.

Similar to paintball, marking pellets break upon impact, marking the target with luminescent liquid. Unlike traditional plastic pellets, marking rounds are heavier to ensure breakage on impact, and their weight can be adjusted by adding heavier liquid.

The significance of marking rounds lies in their ability to allow shooters to observe where they hit the target, enabling them to learn from their mistakes and enhance their accuracy.

Another airsoft invention designed for military training is reusable grenades that imitate the fragmentation of real grenades in war games and scenarios.

The grenade has the ability to be filled with either paint or pellets and is activated through the use of highly pressurized gas that is quickly released to break the shell, dispersing the contents in all directions.

Scott Frank is responsible for designing and creating a grenade that is intended to be as realistic and reliable as an actual grenade. He has incorporated a more precise timing mechanism and additional safety features to prevent unintended discharge.

With the introduction of marking rounds and reusable grenades, airsoft has gained the necessary advancements to be implemented in military and law enforcement training environments.

Airsoft guns utilized for training purposes differ from those designed for civilians. Professional training guns are created to replicate the weight, sensation, and sound of actual firearms.

Generally, these guns are gas blowback (GBB) models, equipped with a weighted blowback mechanism to enhance the recoil force. Alternatively, some are automatic electric guns (AEGs) and are outfitted with a blowback mechanism. Additionally, muzzle protectors are utilized to amplify the sound to a level of decibels similar to that of genuine firearms.

The average FPS (feet per second) for professional training airsoft guns is higher compared to civilian models.

Compared to simulation training, airsoft is a more cost-effective option. According to Benjamin Kratz, the battalion executive officer at Fort Jackson, a single blank M16 round can be as expensive as 32 rounds of airsoft.

Furthermore, airsoft can be utilized to enhance immersion in military simulations conducted in locations like malls or prisons. Various event producers, such as MiR Tactical, organize such events.

Shooting stances & positions

Although there are no real rules for stances in airsoft employing proper positions and techniques can enhance your ability to achieve the best accuracy when shooting a airsoft gun.

It's important to note that these techniques only scratch the surface, and a deeper understanding of additional variables, including wind, heat, can significantly impact your precision.

Shooting Rests
To achieve the highest degree of accuracy when shooting during a game, it's advisable to use a rest.

In case a rest isn't available, you can use a stable object like a log or a large rock. However, it's essential not to rest the barrel of the airsoft rifle directly on a hard surface as it can cause the airsoft rifle to fire higher than usual.

To prevent this, it's recommended to place some padding, such as a hat or a jacket, beneath the airsoft rifle.

Breathing
Proper breathing technique is critical to avoid any movement in the airsoft rifle that can lead to inaccurate shots.

Before pulling the trigger, take a deep breath and exhale about half of it. Hold your breath while gently squeezing the trigger. However, it's important to note that holding your breath for too long can increase your pulse rate and cause the rifle to move.

In such a situation, take another breath and begin the process again. It's natural to feel excited during an airsoft game, which can make it challenging to control your breathing. Therefore, try to remain calm and follow the correct breathing procedure.

Trigger Squeeze
When firing a airsoft gun, jerking or clenching the trigger abruptly can cause the rifle to move, resulting in missed shots.

To avoid this, it's essential to apply slow and steady pressure on the trigger until the gun fires.

It's important to practice this technique to make it a habit along with proper breathing control. This will improve your shooting skills and help you achieve better accuracy.

Follow Through
Following through after firing a shot is crucial to avoid jerking the airsoft gun before the airsoft bb has left the barrel.

It's essential to continue squeezing or maintain the trigger pressure until the bb has exited the barrel.

This technique will improve your shooting accuracy and help you maintain consistency in your shots.

KNEELING

Kneeling

The kneeling position provides less stability than the prone and sitting positions as only one arm is braced to support the shooter.

STANDING

Standing

The most challenging stance for firing an accurate shot is standing without any arm support. Holding the barrel steady in this position is difficult. So focus on limiting the movement of the barrel to a small area and aim for smooth and natural motion to achieve the best shot.

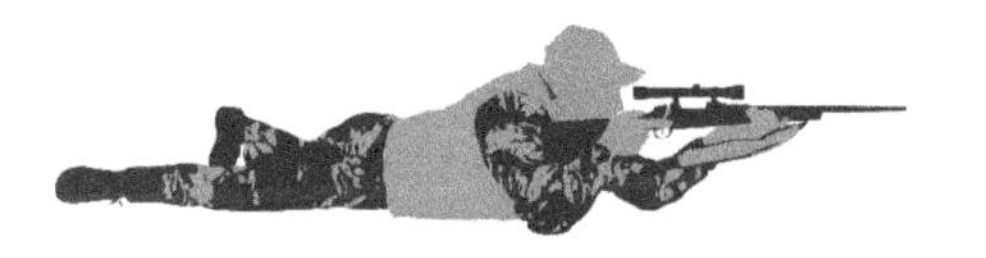

PRONE

Prone

Out of the these positions, the prone position offers the most stability. It is also the easiest to maintain, making it an ideal position for mastering the fundamentals of firing, including breath control, trigger squeeze, aiming, and follow-through.

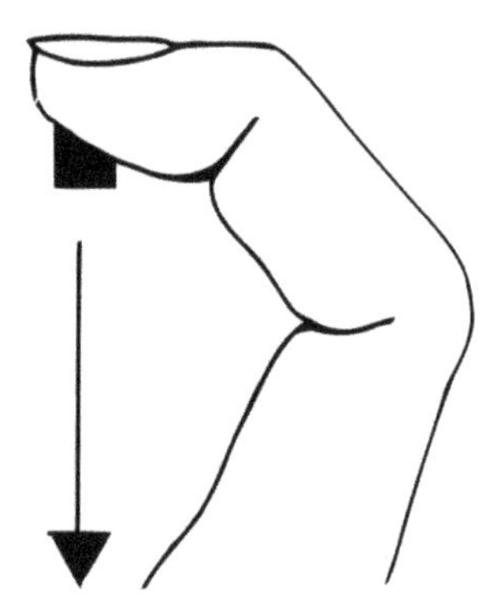

Trigger Control

The image above shows the correct finger placement on the trigger.
Always place the pad of your trigger finger square onto the trigger blade.

Regardless of the type of trigger or method of control, the primary objective is to release the trigger without moving the gun from its point of aim. Any triggering method that consistently achieves this outcome is acceptable.

It's important for the shooter to be able to feel the exact moment the trigger releases and control it precisely during training and competitions. The best trigger weight can vary depending on the shooter, so it's necessary to experiment to find the right setting. To adjust the trigger you may have to experiment with different trigger springs.

To achieve accurate trigger control, the trigger hand must be positioned to allow the trigger finger to pull the trigger blade directly back along the airguns centerline, without pushing the airgun to the left or right.
The hand must also be positioned to prevent any lifting or pulling down on the airgun when the trigger is released.

When holding a rifle, the amount of pressure you use is up to you, but it's a good idea to use the same pressure every time. Don't try to steer the rifle with your right hand. Some people disagree about where to put your thumb on your trigger hand, but as long as you don't move it when you're pulling the trigger, it doesn't really matter where it is.

There have been various ways of describing the proper technique of smoothly increasing the pressure on the trigger until the airgun fires. The commonly used phrase "squeeze the trigger" is a but misleading, as it implies that the whole hand applies pressure, which is not the case. In the correct trigger release, only the trigger finger moves, while the aim remains steady and the gun fires without any extra movement.

When you're releasing the trigger on a gun, a common mistake to avoid is "snatching the trigger" meaning pulling the trigger too quickly and suddenly, This can jerk the gun off its aim point.

After releasing the trigger, the process of maintaining the aim and position of the gun is just as important as the aiming and firing process itself. This is known as follow-through, and it is especially important in rifle shooting because the action is slow. The shot takes time to develop after the trigger is released, so any disturbance in the aim during this period can result in a poor shot.

There are some good reasons to practice good follow-through when shooting a airsoft gun. For example, there's usually a short delay between seeing the right aim and actually pulling the trigger, and during this time, you need to keep aiming the gun to make sure the shot hits the target. You also need to keep your muscles tense and in the same position until the shot has left the gun. If you don't, the gun could move slightly and mess up the shot.

To have good follow-through, you should keep aiming the gun for about a second after you pull the trigger. Some people do it for longer, but that's usually not necessary and can be tiring. You should also stay focused on the shot and watch the gun to see how it moves during and after the shot. This is called "calling the shot" and can help you improve your technique. Following through is really important if you want to shoot accurately and consistently.

Airsoft games types

Skirmish

It's highly probable that you have already participated in a Skirmish or two. However, if you haven't, then this might be your first encounter with Airsoft. Skirmish is the most widely played game type across Airsoft sites on weekends, and it's an excellent way for beginners to get started with the sport. This game type is very basic and beginner friendly, with a range of games played throughout the day, ensuring that everyone is continuously engaged and active without any dull moments.

Airsoft skirmish games can include various types of gameplay modes such as team deathmatch, capture the flag, domination, hostage rescue, and more. The specific games played during a skirmish can vary depending on the site or event organizer.

Milsim

MilSim, short for Military Simulation, is a game mode designed with the aim of providing an immersive experience through realistic Rules of Engagement (RoE). The game mode aims to simulate real-life military scenarios such as operations, patrols, or guard duty, where players can wait half along time without even firing their replica firearms (RIFs) and instead fully immerse themselves in the military simulation. Every player is assigned a specific role and is expected to fulfill their responsibilities throughout the day.

Speedsoft

Airsoft Speedsoft is a fast-paced and competitive game mode that focuses on quick movements, fast reflexes, and close-quarters combat. In Speedsoft, players prioritize speed and agility over realism and typically wear minimalistic gear and clothing to allow for maximum mobility.

Speedsoft gameplay often takes place in smaller indoor arenas with obstacles, such as walls and barrels, that players can use for cover and maneuvering. The objective of the game is usually to eliminate the opposing team or capture a flag.

Players in Speedsoft often use lightweight and high-capacity magazines, allowing them to quickly reload and continue firing. They also typically use compact and lightweight airsoft guns with shorter barrels and high rates of fire.

Airsoft Speedsoft is popular among players who enjoy the adrenaline rush of fast-paced and intense gameplay and the skill required for quick reflexes and accurate shooting in close quarters combat.

Different skirmish games

There are several different skirmish airsoft games, each with its own unique objectives and gameplay.

Here are some of the most common ones:

Team Deathmatch: This is the most basic and popular airsoft game mode. The objective is to eliminate all players on the opposing team. The team with the last surviving player wins the game.

Capture the Flag: Two teams compete to capture the other team's flag and bring it back to their own base. The team with the most flags at the end of the game wins.

Domination: In this game mode, teams compete to control and hold a specific location on the playing field. The team that holds the location for the longest amount of time wins.

Escort: In Escort, one team is tasked with protecting a VIP player while the other team tries to eliminate them. The VIP must be escorted to a designated extraction point, and the team that successfully escorts or eliminates the VIP wins.

Search and Destroy: This game mode is similar to Escort, but instead of a VIP, teams are trying to locate and destroy an objective on the other team's side of the field. The team that destroys the objective or eliminates all opposing players wins.

Last Man Standing: In this game mode, players start as individuals, and the last player standing wins the game. This mode can also be played in teams, with the last team or player standing declared the winner.

King of the Hill: This game mode involves teams competing to capture and control a central point on the field. The team that holds the point for the longest time wins.

Zombies: In this game mode, one or more players start as zombies, and their objective is to eliminate all other players by tagging them. Once a player is tagged, they become a zombie and join the attacking team.

These are just some of the most common airsoft game modes, and there are many variations and combinations of these game modes that can be played.

The rules and objectives of each game mode can also be customized to fit the preferences of the players or the specific playing field.

Airsoft tournaments

There are several major airsoft tournaments and competitions that take place around the world.

Here are some of the most notable ones:

Airsoft Surgeon European Championship: This is one of the biggest airsoft tournaments in Europe, held annually in the UK. It features top players from around the world competing in a variety of different game modes.

Airsoft GI SS Airsoft Invitational: This is an annual tournament held in California, USA, organized by Airsoft GI. It features both professional and amateur teams competing for cash prizes.

American MilSim: This is a series of milsim (Military Simulation) events held across the United States. It focuses on realism and immersive gameplay, with players taking on roles as soldiers and completing objectives in a realistic combat environment.

RedWolf Airsoft Masters: This is an annual airsoft tournament held in Hong Kong, organized by RedWolf Airsoft. It features teams from around the world competing in a variety of different game modes.

SpeedQB: This is a competitive airsoft league that focuses on speed and agility. Teams compete in a fast-paced arena-style environment, with matches lasting only a few minutes.

MILSIM West: This is another series of milsim events held across the United States. It is known for its high level of realism and immersive gameplay, with players taking on roles as soldiers and completing objectives in a realistic combat environment.

Airsoft Action Challenge: This is an annual airsoft tournament held in the UK, organized by Airsoft Action magazine. It features teams from around the world competing in a variety of different game modes.

These are a small sample of the major airsoft tournaments and competitions that take place around the world.

There are many other regional and national tournaments that may be of interest to airsoft players.

Top garden fun airsoft bb guns

BLACKVIPER HEAVYWEIGHT M1911-A1
(SPRING POWERED)

GALAXY - G36 REVOLVER WITH 6"
BARREL
(SPRING POWERED)

GALAXY G51 M&P BIG BIRD FULL METAL
BB GUN
(SPRING POWERED)

SRC SR-645

BLACKVIPER P226 PISTOL
(GAS POWERED)

BLACKVIPER REVOLVER WITH MID SIZE
BARREL
(GAS POWERED)

The airsoft guns depicted were current models available at the time this book was published.

VIGOR L85A1 SA80
(SPRING POWERED)

WELL M16-A3 RIFLE
(SPRING POWERED)

CYMA ZM51 BOLT ACTION SNIPER RIFLE
(SPRING POWERED)

AGM M180-C2 PUMP ACTION SHOTGUN

BLACKVIPER G294 ŠKORPION VZ.61
SUBMACHINE GUN
(CO2 POWERED)

WELL D91 UZI REPLICA BB GUN WITH
FOLDING STOCK
(ELECTRIC POWERED)

The airsoft guns depicted were current models available at the time this book was published.

Airsoft guns for advanced airsoft play

Selecting the optimal airsoft gun could be a challenging endeavor, given the multitude of available models and platforms. This task becomes even more daunting for novices in the Airsoft world, with a plethora of diverse viewpoints existing out there. Whether you're in the market for dependable rifles, distinctive pistols, long-range snipers, room-clearing shotguns, or machine guns, we've compiled a list of our top recommendations to help you get out of your garden and started in advance airsoft play.

Things to think about when buying your airsoft gun.

Airsoft is an entertaining hobby, and airsoft guns should be able to provide joy.

Recoil, sound, design, optional accessories, and overall "coolness" are all important considerations in making a gun exciting. Non-blowback models, such as a revolver with realistic ammunition that can be loaded into a rotating cylinder, is great fun and enjoyable.

Airsoft guns are attractive to many people because they replicate actual firearms. While some manufacturers attempt to reproduce the details and feel of a genuine gun, some are successful, while others are not and create something that is more like a toy.

Power, measured in feet-per-second (FPS), range, and accuracy, with an adjustable hop-up to ensure consistency and precision, are all important in selecting the best airsoft gun for yourself.

Good quality construction, materials, and refinement are important not only in the external components but also internally. How does it feel when you hold it? Does everything fit together well without any gaps in the shell?, Are there any rattles?, Does it have a smooth operation?, and think about how strong each component and durable its is, these should all be taken into consideration.

Airsoft guns that are priced affordably can be rated highly against some of the more expensive models and as price is a crucial consideration for most airsoft players always compare products before deciding on what to go for.

Like most things airsoft guns will deprecate over time and use however occasionally, an airsoft gun stands out simply because it is a one of a kind, either because no one else produces it or because it holds collectible value. It's worth noting that some rare or limited edition airsoft guns even appreciate in value in the secondary market.

Tokyo Marui Hi Capa 5.1
GBB Airsoft Pistol

TOKYO MARUI VSR-10 G-SPEC AIRSOFT SNIPER RIFLE

ASG CZ SCORPION EVO 3 AEG

UMAREX GLOCK 17 GEN 5
GBB AIRSOFT PISTOL

RWA AGENCY ARMS EXA
AIRSOFT PISTOL

SILVERBACK TAC41P BOLT ACTION RIFLE

The airsoft guns depicted were current models available at the time this book was published.

GHK M4 GBBR AR15

SIG SAUER M17 (P320)

Army R26 1911

ARES AMOEBA TACTICAL 'STRIKER' AST-01 SNIPER RIFLE

H&K G3A3 GBB rifle (UMAREX Licensed)

DOUBLE EAGLE P80 GBB PISTOL

The airsoft guns depicted were current models available at the time this book was published.

Springfield Armory XDM 3.8 Gas Blowback Pistol

HFC Stealth Assassin SOCOM MK23 Gas pistol with silencer

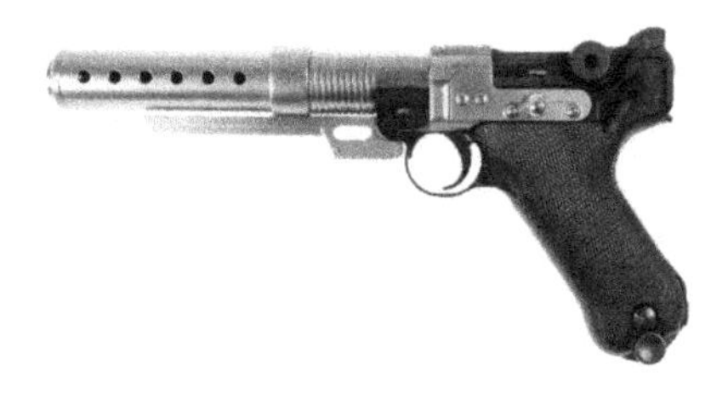

Armorer Works Rebel A180 Gasblowback Pistol

Jag Precision x Taran Tactical International Licensed JW4 Pit Viper

WE XDM IPSC Special Edition Gas Blowback Pistol

Army Custom 34 Series Gas Blowback Pistol

The airsoft guns depicted were current models available at the time this book was published.

Marushin Raptor Zero 1892 Tactical Winchester Under Lever Gas Shotgun Black

Golden Eagle M4A1 Gas Blowback Rifle

KWA M11A1 GBB

Novritsch Airsoft – SSX303 Stealth Gas Rifle

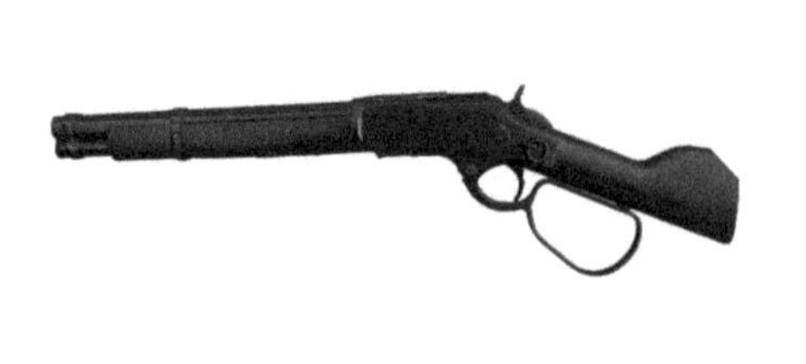

KTW Winchester 1873 (Randall – Short)

FN Herstal Scar-H Gas Blowback Rifle

The airsoft guns depicted were current models available at the time this book was published.

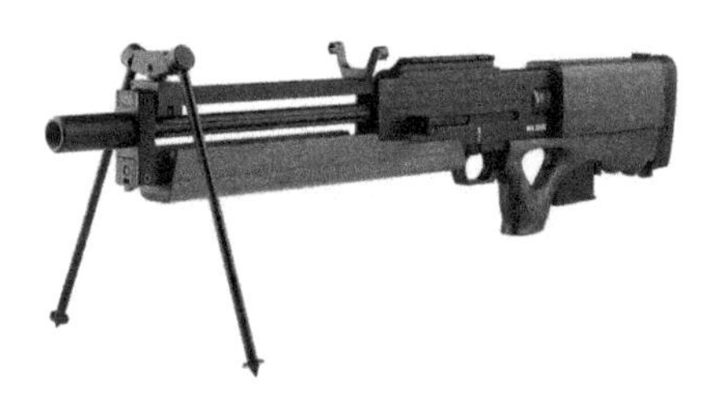

Tokyo Marui VSR-ONE Sniper Rifle

Ares WA2000 Spring Powered Sniper Rifle (Real Wood – Bipod – SR-018)

Double Eagle SAKO TRG M10 Sniper Rifle Spring Bolt Action M67

Saigo Defence Kyudo 04 Sniper Rifle Spring Metal Polymer Black

Double Bell VSR-10 Sniper Rifle with Scope and Bipod

Double Bell KAR98K WWII Faux Wood

The airsoft guns depicted were current models available at the time this book was published.

Other airsoft equiptment

Svoboda M94A4 Mortar Co2 Powered

Double Bell AK Series 40mm Under-Barrel Grenade Launcher

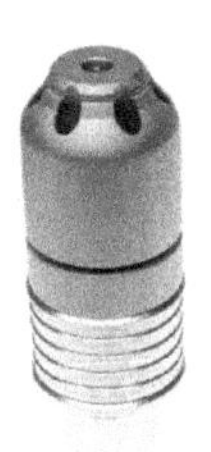

Double Bell Moscart Gas Grenade 36 Rounds

Cloud 9 Ring Pull Grenade Green Disc

Cloud 9 Ring Pull Grenade Red Disc

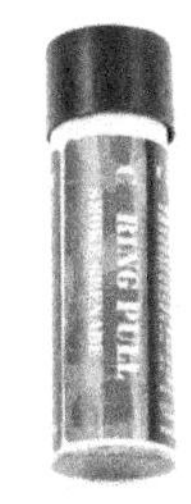

Cloud 9 Ring Pull Grenade White Disc

Viper Tactical Security Patrol Belt System

Kombat M1 Helmet

Nuprol Balaclava Shield Mask

The airsoft products depicted are current models that were available at the time this book was published.

Viper Tactical Neck Gaiter

KombatUK Tactical Pro All Leather Patrol Boot

Jack Pyke LLCS 3D Concealment Suit

Kombatuk Operators Mesh Top

Highlander Kids British Camo Combat trousers

KombatUK ACU Shirt BTP Camo

KombatUK Alpha Tactical Gloves

KombatUK Full Face Mesh Mask

Nuprol Mesh Goggles Grey

The airsoft products depicted are current models that were available at the time this book was published.

Swiss Arms Micro Laser Sight

Nuprol TECH M1K Red Dot Sight

Walther Competition 3 Point Sight

Nuprol Hand Signal Sights

Hawke Fast Mount 4x32 Mil-Dot Scope

Richter Optik Exact Scope 4x32 Compact AOE

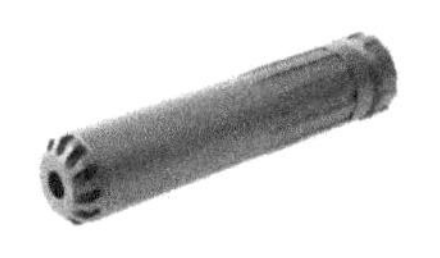

Action Army AAP-01 DDW Suppressor 14mm CCW Black

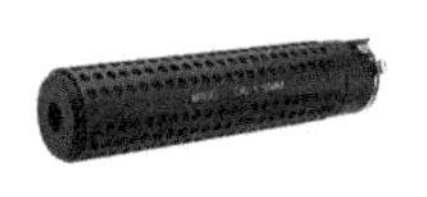

GK Tactical KAC QD Suppressor with SR16 Flash Hider

Big Foot 470 Rd M4 Style Speed Loader

F.A.Q

1. What is airsoft?

Airsoft is a recreational activity where participants use replica firearms that shoot plastic pellets called BBs.

2. Is airsoft safe?

Airsoft can be safe if proper safety measures are taken, such as wearing protective gear and following the rules of the game.

3. What equipment do I need to play airsoft?

To play airsoft, you will need a Airsoft gun, BBs, protective gear, and possibly other accessories such as a holster, extra magazines & CO2 or green gas.

4. What are the different types of airsoft guns?

There are several types of airsoft guns, including spring-powered, gas-powered, and electric-powered guns.

5. How do I maintain my airsoft gun?

To maintain your airsoft gun, you should clean it regularly, lubricate it as needed, and store it properly.

6. What are the rules of airsoft?

The rules of airsoft vary depending on the game and location, but generally, players must wear protective gear and follow rules regarding shooting distance, firing mode, and safety.

7. How do I get started in airsoft?

To get started in airsoft, you can find local airsoft groups or events, purchase equipment, and practice safety and gameplay techniques.

8. What are some popular airsoft games?

Some popular airsoft games include capture the flag, team deathmatch, and objective-based games such as hostage rescue or bomb defusal.

9. Is airsoft legal?

Airsoft is legal in most countries, but there may be restrictions on the sale, ownership, or use of airsoft guns in certain areas.

10. What is the difference between airsoft and paintball?

Airsoft uses replica firearms that shoot BBs, while paintball uses guns that shoot paint-filled pellets. Airsoft is typically played with more realistic equipment and gameplay, while paintball is often more casual and focused on elimination-style games.

Venues to play airsoft

1. The Mall	Reading
2. Tier 1 Military Simulation	Essex
3. Apocalypse Airsoft	Kent
4. Red 1 Airsoft	Herefordshire
5. Urban Assault	Glasgow
6. UCAP Airsoft	Portsmouth
7. First and Only Airsoft	Manchester
8. Ambush Adventures	Surrey
9. Skirmish Airsoft	Birmingham
10. The Gaol	Oakham
11. Halo Mill Proving Grounds	Huddersfield
12. Spartan Airsoft	East Sussex
13. Dragon's Lair Airsoft	Northampton
14. Ground Zero Airsoft	Bicester
15. Gunman Airsoft	Eversley
16. The Department CQB	Bristol
17. Warzone Airsoft	Essex
18. Bunker 51	London
19. Elite Action Games	Hampshire
20. Alpha 55	Nottingham
21. Area 51	Hertfordshire
22. Bravo One Airsoft	West Midlands
23. Xsite Airsoft	West Yorkshire
24. Black Ops Cribbs Causeway	Bristol
25. Anzio Camp	Leek

More on the next page>>>

26. Camp Sparta	Nottingham
27. Tac House Spartan	Kidderminster
28. Apocalypse Paintball and Airsoft	East Sussex
29. Newbury Airsoft	Berkshire
30. The Fort	Staffordshire
31. Phoenix Airsoft	East Sussex
32. Strikeforce CQB	Gloucestershire
33. Elite Action Games	Essex
34. Elite Airsoft	Derbyshire
35. Airsoft Plantation	Kent
36. Extreme Airsoft	Cheshire
37. Urban Assault	Cardiff
38. Helmand Valley Gun Club	Shropshire
39. Gunman Airsoft	Norwich
40. Battle Lakes	East Sussex
41. Airsoft Edinburgh	Edinburgh
42. Zed Adventures	High Wycombe
43. Apocalypse Airsoft	Cambridgeshire
44. Paintball and Airsoft Battlezone	Kent
45. Kingsley Wood	Staffordshire
46. Ironsight Airsoft	Northampton
47. Skirmish Airsoft Billericay	Essex
48. Project X Airsoft	Essex
49. Strikeforce CQB	Gloucestershire
50. Ambush Adventures	Surrey

Please note that this is not an exhaustive list, and there may be many other great airsoft sites in the UK that I haven't mentioned.

Airsoft retailers in the UK

Here is a list of some online airsoft retailers in the UK:

1. **Patrol Base** - https://www.patrolbase.co.uk/ Patrol Base is a popular UK-based airsoft retailer, offering a wide range of airsoft guns, accessories, and gear. They have a large selection of brands and products, and offer free UK delivery on orders over £50.

2. **Zero One Airsoft** - https://www.zerooneairsoft.com/ Zero One Airsoft is another popular airsoft retailer in the UK, offering a wide range of airsoft guns, accessories, and gear. They have a large selection of brands and products, and offer free UK delivery on orders over £100.

3. **Land Warrior Airsoft** - https://www.landwarriorairsoft.com/ Land Warrior Airsoft is a Scotland-based airsoft retailer, offering a wide range of airsoft guns, accessories, and gear. They have a large selection of brands and products, and offer free UK delivery on orders over £50.

4. **Airsoft World** - https://www.airsoftworld.net/ Airsoft World is a UK-based airsoft retailer, offering a wide range of airsoft guns, accessories, and gear. They have a large selection of brands and products, and offer free UK delivery on orders over £50.

5. **Action Hobbies** - https://www.actionhobbies.co.uk/ Action Hobbies is a UK-based airsoft retailer, offering a wide range of airsoft guns, accessories, and gear. They have a large selection of brands and products, and offer free UK delivery on orders over £100.

6. **Socom Tactical Airsoft** - https://www.socomtactical.net/ Socom Tactical Airsoft is a UK-based airsoft retailer, offering a wide range of airsoft guns, accessories, and gear. They have a large selection of brands and products, and offer free UK delivery on orders over £100.

7. **JD Airsoft** - https://jdairsoft.net/ JD Airsoft is a UK-based airsoft retailer, offering a wide range of airsoft guns, accessories, and gear. They have a large selection of brands and products, and offer free UK delivery on orders over £100.

8. **Pro Airsoft Supplies** - https://www.proairsoftsupplies.co.uk/ Pro Airsoft Supplies is a UK-based airsoft retailer that offers a wide range of airsoft guns, accessories, and gear. They have a large selection of products from well-known brands, and offer free UK delivery on orders over £50.

9. **Airsoft Direct** - https://www.airsoftdirect.co.uk/ Airsoft Direct is a UK-based airsoft retailer that offers a wide range of airsoft guns, accessories, and gear. They have a large selection of products from well-known brands, and offer free UK delivery on orders over £50.

10. **Wolf Armouries** - https://www.wolfarmouries.co.uk/ Wolf Armouries is a UK-based airsoft retailer that offers a wide range of airsoft guns, accessories, and gear. They have a large selection of products from well-known brands, and offer free UK delivery on orders over £100.

More on the next page>>>

11. BBguns4less - https://bbguns4less.co.uk/ BBguns4less is a UK-based airsoft and BB gun retailer that offers a wide range of products for airsoft and BB gun enthusiasts. They have a large selection of products at affordable prices, and offer free UK delivery on orders over £50.

12. Just BB Guns - https://www.justbbguns.co.uk/ Just BB Guns is a UK-based retailer that offers a wide range of airsoft guns, accessories, and gear, as well as BB guns. They have a large selection of products at affordable prices, and offer free UK delivery on orders over £50.

13. Airsoft Zone - https://www.airsoftzone.co.uk/ Airsoft Zone is a UK-based airsoft retailer that offers a wide range of airsoft guns, accessories, and gear. They have a large selection of products from well-known brands, and offer free UK delivery on orders over £100.

14. Airsoft Monkey - https://www.airsoftmonkey.co.uk/ Airsoft Monkey is a UK-based airsoft retailer that offers a wide range of airsoft guns, accessories, and gear. They have a large selection of products from well-known brands, and offer free UK delivery on orders over £100.

15. Airsoft Guns UK - https://www.airsoftgunsuk.co.uk/ Airsoft Guns UK is a UK-based airsoft retailer that offers a wide range of airsoft guns, accessories, and gear. They have a large selection of products from well-known brands, and offer free UK delivery on orders over £50.

16. Airsoft International - https://www.ai-mag.com/ Airsoft International is a UK-based airsoft magazine that also offers an online store. They have a large selection of airsoft guns, accessories, and gear, as well as a range of airsoft-related books and magazines.

17. Blades and Bows - https://www.bladesandbows.co.uk/ Blades and Bows is a UK-based retailer that offers a wide range of products for outdoor enthusiasts, including airsoft guns and accessories. They have a large selection of products from well-known brands, and offer free UK delivery on orders over £100.

18. Airsoft Objectives - https://www.airsoftobjectives.co.uk/ Airsoft Objectives is a UK-based airsoft retailer that offers a wide range of airsoft guns, accessories, and gear. They have a large selection of products from well-known brands, and offer free UK delivery on orders over £50.

19. Airsoft Arms - https://www.airsoftarms.eu/ Airsoft Arms is a UK-based airsoft retailer that offers a wide range of airsoft guns, accessories, and gear.

20. Crawley Surplus Store - https://www.surplusstore.co.uk/ based in the UK. They offer a wide range of airsoft guns, accessories, and gear, as well as airguns and military surplus items. They have been in business for over 25 years and offer both online shopping and a physical store location in Crawley, West Sussex. They also offer free UK delivery on orders over £100.

This list is not comprehensive, and there are numerous excellent airsoft retailers, both online and with physical stores, that are not included here.

A special thank you to the following people who either helped with the creation of content for this book or have support the products and helped with research, without these people this book would have not been possible:

Sportsmarketing
Nuprol
Unsplash
BEAR Labs
Michał Franczak
Specna Arms
Daniel Balaure
Scott Graham
Toxic Player
Black Cat
FBS
Freepik
petrex
Enola Gaye
MP40 Model Guns
MAXX
Milbro
Blackviper
Galaxy
SRC
Well
Vigor
CYMA
AGM
Blig Foot
Delta
Acetech
BO Manufacture
Umarex
Abbey
Swiss Arms

Disclaimer

As the authors and publishers of this book, we have made every effort to ensure that the information contained within these pages is accurate and up-to-date. We have meticulously researched and fact-checked each detail, striving to provide our readers with the most reliable information available. However, despite our best efforts, we cannot guarantee that every piece of information presented in this book is entirely free from error. As such, we must emphasize that we are not liable for any inaccuracies or omissions that may be present. We encourage readers to exercise their own judgement and seek out additional sources to verify the information presented here. That being said, we stand by the veracity of our research and firmly believe that the information contained within these pages is as correct as can be. We hope that our readers find this book to be a valuable resource and trust that they will use the information presented here responsibly and with care.

Ingram Content Group UK Ltd.
Milton Keynes UK
UKHW020712260523
422386UK00010B/32

Inseparable:
Granny and Grandad's Autobiographies

By Leonard and Catherine Williams

Janet Todd

and Matthew Hall

Dedicated to our wonderful grandchildren

Eddie, Max, Kate, Harriet,

Rosie, Georgia, Thomas,

Izzy and Imogen

Published by
Gilbert Knowle Publishers
6 Valeside
Durham DH1 4RF
England

ISBN: 978-1-9998871-6-2

"...snorkelling and swimming among the fishes in the coral reef" (p. 63).

When Catherine asked me if I might illustrate and publish the autobiographies that she and Leonard had written, I immediately said yes. I knew, of course, that Janet's introduction about the Todd family and Catherine's account of her life would be of great interest. But even more was I looking forward to seeing what Leonard had written for his grandchildren. Len was a brilliant conversationalist. He was superb in argument, his stories were very funny, and his discussions of medicine were compelling, as were his insights into the human psyche. This fascinating autobiography gives some indication of the sparkle that Len created when he spoke. However, the law being what it is, I have also found it prudent to make some cuts.

Peter Hayes

Contents

Autobiography of Leonard Hugh Paul Williams

24 January 1945 – 19 December 2022

Introduction

When Leonard retired, he received a farewell card from one of his colleagues. He kept this card and the following is a quotation from that card:

> *It has been a privilege working with you for the last 20+ years. It has been entertaining and enlightening in equal measure. We will miss your insightful and incisive comments at the meetings. As Jonathan Swift said: "When a true genius appears in the world, you may know him by this sign, that the dunces are all in confederacy against him".*

For Better or Worse

Chapter 1
My beginnings

I was born in Castlewellan in the north of Ireland on 24th January 1945. My mother, Anne Josephine, was 34 years old. She was living with her parents, Dr Hugh John and Mary McNabb. My elder brother Vincent was 2 years 8 months older than me. My father was at sea in a war ship at the time. This was a few months after D Day.

I was born in my grandparents' house, as was Vincent. It was a large lovely house which had been the home of my grandparents and their 8 children for many years. The house faced towards the Mountains of Mourne, a range of beautiful mountains, just 4 miles away. There were clear views to the mountains from every front window. The back windows looked towards Bunkers Hill. Later, I grew to love Castlewellan and this house.

The following day, I made my first appearance in public. I was taken to the very grand Catholic church in Castlewellan to be christened and I became Leonard Hugh Paul; Leonard was my father's brother, Hugh my grandfather and one of his children and I don't know where Paul came from.

I lived in the House in Castlewellan until I was about 20 months old, when my mother and us two children moved to Pank Avenue in New Barnet. Barnet was a newish dormitory town on the northern edge of London lacking in any interesting features or attractions but nonetheless rather ordinarily nice.
I have no memory of any of this.

Chapter 2
My family

Family has a tremendous influence on the life of any child and so it is necessary to know the family.

My mother Anne or, as she was often known, Annie, was the most important influence. She was born in our house in Castlewellan on 18th January 1911. Her father was a successful well-respected family doctor. She was the fourth child. The third child, Malachy, died when he was a baby and my grandmother became severely depressed after this. This is likely to have harmed her ability to care for my mother. However, my mother always spoke kindly about her, saying her husband was impatient and unkind to her for the rest of her life.

The "Irish Troubles" were growing. Ireland at that time was part of Britain but most of the Irish people were Catholics and wanted independence from England. The Catholics attacked the British institutions in Ireland and the British responded brutally; many Irish "freedom fighters" were executed or "martyred for Ireland". Later, the English sent a military type police force called the Black and Tans to enforce order. These were largely ex-soldiers from the first world war and were even more brutal in their suppression of the Catholic uprising, particularly in the summary execution of agitators. The McNabbs were drawn into this conflict.

A young Catholic protestor called Jimmy Johnson was shot in the chest in Castlewellan. He was brought to our house and my grandfather operated on him on our kitchen table to remove the bullet and stop the bleeding. The north of Ireland was a predominantly Protestant area of Ireland and many of the Protestants were angry with my grandfather for saving Jimmy. Many stopped seeing him and therefore paying him when they needed medical help. They simply went to other doctors in other towns. He had been an important person in Castlewellan on the town committees and so forth but all this was taken away from him.

This carried on for years and indeed is still carrying on. Much later, during the second world war, two of my mother's brothers were imprisoned for joining the IRA; my uncles Joe and Hugh

.

It is not surprising that my mother's early childhood was unsettling. Her early school years were unhappy and she was thought stupid by the teachers. And in those days children really were told they were stupid by teachers and were beaten with canes for being stupid. She was sent to secondary school in Kilkeel, a town about 20 miles from Castlewellan but again she failed in her studies. I don't know if she boarded at Kilkeel or travelled there and back every day by bus. That would have taken several hours each day. When she was a young woman, she decided to become a Catholic nun. Her family and the rest of the Catholic community in Castlewellan would have been immensely proud of her and would have celebrated her choice. When she entered the convent, a great ceremony called a coronation was held on her behalf. She was crowned as a servant of god. She went to live in a convent. She would have had to pray many times a day and study religion. She had to remain silent for much of the time. Unhappily, she could not cope with life in the convent and decided to leave. This brought great shame on her. She never ever talked about this part of her life. On one occasion I found a photograph in our house in Castlewellan of a young woman in what I thought to be a wedding dress. I brought it to another room to ask my mother, grandfather and Aunt Peggy about it. Peggy said it was my mother's coronation celebration for her admission to the convent. My mother flew into a rage, took the photo from me, told me I was wicked and that I was never to mention this ever again.

When she left the convent she also had to leave Castlewellan. She went to Derry to train as a hotel worker.

All this happened before I was born and I cannot be sure about much of it. But a lot of it is correct. When I or others talk about my mother's weaknesses and inadequacies, I will often defend her. She did not have the easiest childhood.

My father was called Joseph Oswald Williams and was known as Joe. He also had an interesting upbringing. His father died of pneumonia well before I was born. I think he may have been a teacher and I think he may have been a Methodist preacher as well. I imagine he was a rather good kind man who studied a lot and would be thought of as a very decent respectable man, probably boring and bookish. Joe's mother, my grandmother, was called May Elizabeth. She was a teacher and ran her own private infants' school in Finchley. They had 4 children, Leonard, Elizabeth who was always known as Sissy, Dora and lastly Joe. Grandma and the children were immensely proud of Leonard because he went to Oxford University and became a Methodist minister. It was never mentioned that he became an alcoholic and left the church. Sissy was nice enough, a spinster and ever so boring. She and grandma liked to call me Tootles; agh! Dora was even more boring. However, even Dora could not match her husband, another Leonard, for boringness. Leonard and Dora had a daughter called Elizabeth and she was ……. yes, you've guessed it!

Joe did not do well at school and he left at 16 to join the merchant navy with the Shaw Saville line. He did well and he quickly became a deck officer. However, around the year 1936, he started becoming interested in the Catholic religion. He decided to leave the navy and train as a Catholic priest. He was inspired by Father Vincent McNabb, about whom, I will write more later on.

However, his plan was interrupted by the onset of World War 2. He joined the RNR, the Royal Navy Reserves. He started in submarines but was soon promoted to Lieutenant and given a surface ship to command, the Northern Dawn. He was stationed in Derry. The sailors were allowed a couple of days off between each sortie to relax and they would go into Derry City. One day Joe went into the Metropole Hotel in Derry for a drink. He noticed the receptionist who was called Anne McNabb. He explained that he had known a priest called Father Vincent McNabb who he greatly admired. Anne replied, "Oh, he's my uncle!!!" They fell in love and decided to get married. The marriage took place in St Malachy's Catholic Church in Castlewellan on the 21st August 1941. Joe was dressed in formal naval uniform, including wearing the sword that sea captains are expected to wear. I have been told that two of Annie's brothers attended the ceremony, shackled to prison officers, because they had been imprisoned for joining the IRA which was fighting for independence from Britain. Annie, aka Ma, subsequently said that is not correct.

Vincent was born 9 months later, on the 31st May 1942. He was called Vincent after Father Vincent. Father Vincent wrote a book called "The Craft of Suffering". That "craft" was certainly practiced by my mother and her family.

After the war, Joe rejoined the Merchant Navy and in due course was promoted to the rank of Captain. For the rest of his working life he sailed large ocean liners to and from New Zealand and Australia, the round trip taking about 3 months. His ship would be docked in England for 3 or 4 weeks. He would spend the first week supervising the unloading, then have 2 weeks off on holiday, usually at home, and then the last week reloading exports bound for Australia and New Zealand.

This meant that Annie was a single mother for about 9 months each year and that they were together for only about 40 complete days each year. This created a great problem between them. She ran and was responsible for everything when he was away, and in general I thought she coped well. She always looked forward to Joe's return and we used to sing about Daddy coming home. But the joy didn't last long. When Joe returned, he found it hard not to take charge, and boy, did she resent this. He was tight with money, preferring to save to buy a bigger and better house, while she had to take in lodgers to supplement the money which he would spend in the pubs and on whiskey.

Also, he liked visiting his family who lived nearby. Ma never liked them but had to tolerate them. They were happy to give her "good advice" and she felt that they were looking down on her as an Irish peasant. She of course had no friends of her own in England to begin with.

Mary was born on 12th January 1947 shortly after we moved to Barnet. I was one year, nearly 2 and Vincent was 4 years 7 months old.

It was very, very hard for her.

Chapter 3
My earliest memories

I am not certain if my earliest memory was in England or Ireland. We used to spend each long summer holiday in Castlewellan, so my time-line is muddled.

My first memory in Pank Avenue was watching Annie singing “daddy’s coming home” with Mary bouncing contentedly on her knee and everybody seeming very happy.

My first memory in Ireland was being in my Aunt Fanny’s house in Belfast watching her children playing on the floor. This would have been a visit as we were on our way to Castlewellan, so I would have been 3 ½ or 4 ½. Again, it was a happy memory.

Chapter 4
Castlewellan

One of my earliest memory in Castlewellan was watching Ging, my grandmother whose real name was, I think, Mary, walking slowly down our poorly lit hall towards me. She was dressed in dark sombre clothes and looked too broad for her height. She didn't say anything and she didn't smile; she didn't even seem to notice me. I don't remember her ever saying anything to me. I was not frightened of her but I could not like her. I just ignored and avoided her, as did everyone else.

My grandfather, Dote, was completely different. He was about 82 at the time. He liked walking with Vincent and me. Every day he would put on his big black boots and get his wooden walking stick and then call us. We nearly always went on the same walk. We walked up through the town into the Domain which was a large country estate owned by Lord Ansley. In there, there was a large lake, teeming with fishes and tadpoles. We would often see newts and frogs. Dote would talk to us about the wildlife and the trees and weeds. It was not a formal estate and there were no flower beds. There were bullocks grazing in the large meadow areas.

After we visited the lake, we would set off up a small mountain called Slieve n'Slat. We walked up past the "great house", through the lower slopes of the climb which was blanketed in pine trees, towards the upper slopes which were covered with coarse grasses and bracken. It was a hard walk but the view from the top towards Slieve Donard was magnificent. I loved it. Dote seemed to me to know so much about nature and was pleased to tell us about it.

He was a well-connected cultured man. He was friends with W. B. Yeats, the famous Nobel prize winning Irish poet. I was not impressed or interested. But much later when my mother came to live in Highland Grove, I learned more about Yeats from her. Ma loved poetry and would repeatedly recite verses from the great poets. She told me that Yeats would visit the house in Castlewellan with his girlfriend, Maud Gonne, and their dog Pug. Ma liked listening to Yeats' poems, and she liked playing with Pug. But most of all, she liked talking to Maud. I asked your granny to read up about Maude; quite a woman in many ways!

As I said before, Dote was a family doctor and he would tell about his work, about how things were in Castlewellan before the NHS was introduced in 1947. He described people dying because they didn't have enough money to pay him. Others would pay him with a dozen eggs or a sack of logs. I saw these people coming to consult him in our house, but, by this time, he was being paid by the NHS. He also took Vincent and me with him when he did house visits to these poor folk. He would call a taxi and we would drive off to some cottage far away in the surrounding countryside. It was humbling to see the tiny hovels in which these poor peasant people lived, with their well-kept vegetable patches, their small orchards and their chicken runs. Tuberculosis was common; this area of County Down was referred to as the Vale of Consumption. As a matter of some interest to me, I had a bad cough when I was in Ireland. And Vincent repeatedly told me I was going to die of it. Well, when I was 13 years old, I had the six-needle test to see if I should have the TB jab, and was told that I did not need it because I was already immune to TB. That meant nothing to me at the time. However, when I went to Canada I had a pre-employment medical examination and again the TB test was strongly positive. The consultant suggested that I be treated for TB on a prophylactic basis but I said I would prefer to wait to see if any symptoms arose. He said in that case, I should have a chest X-ray every 5 years and any time I have a cough that persists for more than one month. And that is what I do. It is well known to medics that about 50% of children who are infected with TB overcome the infection naturally and that recurrence in later life can occur, especially in young adults and the elderly. Many children, and adults, died of TB in the area. So, keep an eye on me!

Dote's favourite story was about Jimmy Johnson being operated on our wooden table in the pantry. (I always found the word pantry to be confusing. In England our pantry was a small food cupboard off the kitchen. In Ireland, it was a large room off the kitchen in which food was prepared.) Jimmy Johnston was a young Catholic agitator, fighting for the independence of Ireland. I guess the year was 1920 or so. Anyway, Jimmy was busy agitating and he was being hunted by the Black and Tans and the police. They caught sight of him in a wood and fired at him. They could not find his body so they presumed they had missed and he escaped. In fact, he had been shot in the chest and had managed to hide. Later, his comrade came and rescued him. He needed medical attention but he would not dare go to hospital, so he was brought secretly to our house. Dote opened his chest and removed the bullet and he recovered. The police found out in due course what had happened. Dote was vilified in the papers. He was ordered off the District Council and all his Protestant patients transferred to other doctors. Dote changed from being an important person in Castlewellan to being the doctor only for the poor Catholics of the area.

Dote lived with his youngest child, a daughter, called Peggy. Aunt Peggy was not married, aged about 35 when I was first aware of her, very religious going to church twice every day, very funny and a bit of a tease, and she argued endlessly with my mother which often ended with both of them in tears. I liked Peggy; she was cheeky. She told me that I walked like a girl, wiggling my bottom. I was outraged but she just kept repeating it and laughing at me which made me furious. It took me a long time to decide that she was only saying it in order to make me mad. I thought her food was good and her fruit cake outstanding, much better than my mother's, but I would not dare say that. Anyway, I thought my mother's cooking was very good and many of her dishes much better than Peggy's.

The house was dominated by Catholicism. I had to go to mass every Sunday and often more than that. I had to go to confession every two weeks and the day after confession I took Holy Communion. Every evening we said the rosary together. I liked to get a window seat so I could look towards the countryside and the Mourne Mountains. (The glass picture in our patio in Highland Grove just outside the kitchen window is that very view.) I also liked looking at the grown-ups faces while saying their rosary. They would have a devout, rather pained expression as if they were trying to be at one with Jesus and share his suffering. I got told to concentrate on my prayers when I was caught watching them, so I had to be careful. I practiced putting on that expression and it came in useful from time to time. I don't think I did not believe in god at that time; I simply did not take the trouble to think about it and was just not interested.

Vincent and I would also go for walks by ourselves. One special walk was down the Cow Lane. This was a lane off the main Castlewellan to Newcastle road. It was an unmade-up farm track and, as the name suggests, covered in cow dung. Halfway down the lane was a little cottage in which a woman lived alone. I had been told she was a bad woman because she had had a baby out of wedlock. She had lost an arm in a farming accident and it was implied that this was just rewards for her sins. I felt sorry for her because I knew that I too was a sinner. She never seemed to be outside her cottage but the garden was always well kept and stocked with vegetables and chickens.

We passed this cottage on our way down to the Burn River. Vincent and I used to explore the waters, trying to catch the fish and anything else that took our fancy. The blackberries there were outstanding, probably because they were well manured by the cattle in the adjacent fields and because nobody else went there. On one occasion, when I was returning alone from the river, I saw the lady in the cottage. She saw me looking at her and she turned away. I ran away but I don't know why. I thought she looked like an ordinary lady and she did not look bad to me. I would have liked to be her friend. I began to think about who is good and who is bad. And from there to, are Protestants really bad as I have been told? The English ones seemed OK. Uncle John was a Protestant. Were the Germans we fought in the war really bad men? You will remember Joe's account of his escort duties in the Atlantic and how he helped to trap a German U-boat. Many of the films in the cinemas at that time were about the nice Brits defeating the horrid Germans.

I had one good friend of my own in Castlewellan. His name was Paddy Burns and he was about 16. I was about 7 when we first met. Paddy worked for Hannatys. Hannaty was the family name of a local butcher's shop, a dairy and a small farm. Paddy was employed to bring the cows to and from the dairy each morning and evening. To begin with, I used to see him driving his herd past our front garden. If I was in the front garden he would chat and after a while he invited me to help him. We drove the cows from their field at the bottom of Cow Lane to the dairy to be milked and then back to their pasture. The cows shared their field with chickens, some of which were in pens and others ran wild in the fields. Paddy taught me how to herd and drive the cows, how to milk them and how to pass the milk through the pasteurising machine. I learnt how to collect the eggs from the chickens and how to search for the wild chickens' nests. I killed some of the chickens by wringing their necks or chopping their heads off. We brought them back to be sold in the shop.

I met up with Paddy for several consecutive summer holidays. He was responsible for some of the trouble I got into. You will remember the story about driving the bullocks onto railway waggons to be taken away. One went to the far end of the holding area. I was asked to go and drive him back towards the station. I went up behind him and gave a whack on the rump with my cane. He kicked out with his back legs and nearly took my head off. He didn't touch me but his hooves missed my face by a whisker or two.

Another time I cycled down to Ballylough because I liked fishing there. I tied two big logs together and paddled out into the lake. It was a dangerous thing to do but I came to no harm. The lake was deep and I could not swim at the time. I also tried "fishing" for ducks. I tied a fishing line to a wooden cotton reel, a garden pea was attached with a fishing hook as bait. I hoped a duck would take the bait, get the hook stuck in his mouth and I could draw him in and wring his neck. The ducks were not tempted and we never had duck for dinner. I now think it would have been unkind.

Castlewellan was great for me; so different from dull suburban London. It was so earthy and life was so close to nature; pity about the religion.

I last visited Castlewellan about 20 years ago with Granny, Vincent and Helen, and Mary and Joe. It had hardly changed but times had moved on.

The resurgence of the "troubles" started in the 1960s. The Catholics and the Protestants had always kept apart in N. Ireland but then they began to fight each other. Hundreds on both sides were murdered. The British army was brought in to quell the trouble but did about as much to inflame it. Finally, a truce was agreed which has been reasonably successful up to the present. We were welcomed in Castlewellan because all the Catholics had known and respected Dote and would have known Ma. A monument had been erected in the town square opposite the Catholic church since I had last been in Castlewellan. It was dedicated to those brave Catholics who had died in the troubles. It was financed by the church and, in particular, by the parish priest, a Father Austen McNabb. Father Austen was Dote's cousin and therefore related to me. We were proudly told that Father Austen was a lovely old man with a twinkle in his eye and that it was he who smuggled the Catholic yobs over the border to murder Protestants and to blow up the Castlewellan police station. I felt no pride in being related to Father Austen.

We were introduced to the owners of our old house. He was the SDLP MP for South Down. He showed us around the house. It seemed so clean and tidy and not like the mess when I was there. He explained that it had been damaged when the police station opposite had been blown up by the IRA. The SDLP party is a non-sectarian party working for unity throughout Northern Ireland. He told us that he had to have bullet proof windows installed in the house. It was lovely talking to him and his wife and revisiting the bedroom in which I was born. I sent him copies of some photos of our family enjoying ourselves in the old house. He is exactly the sort of person that is needed in the Stormont Parliament.

Chapter 5
Life at home in Pank Avenue in the early days and the beginnings of school

Vincent was the most important person in my life in those early days. We used to play together and we slept in the same double bed. He went off to school in the morning while I would play in the house and the garden. I liked digging holes in the garden pretending that I was digging my way down to Australia. Every attempt was thwarted by the hole filling with water and I never understood why. This used to annoy my mother because she tried to keep the garden tidy but she was also pleased that I was out of her way. Life seemed good to my mind but I was always aware that I had to be good or else she would beat me with a leather strap. I was always in minor trouble for being dirty and scruffy. I rarely cleaned my teeth and didn't like washing. I began to get an interest and skill in tending the garden and over the years I learnt a lot about it from Ma. It was one way for her and I to be friends, rather than me being one of her chores.

You have to realise that a woman's life in those days was very different from today. We did not have central heating, just coal fires; no washing machines for clothes or dishes; clothes were dried on an outsides line or with the creel (as Granny calls it) in the kitchen, no fridge, no TV, no microwave, nor a vacuum cleaner etc. In fact, the only electric things in our kitchen were a cooking stove and a kettle. We didn't have a car, so my mother had to take us shopping most days and we had to carry heavy shopping bags back home. England was recovering from WW2 and there were shortages of essentials in the shops. Many foods were rationed. I did not know what a banana was because few were imported into England at that time. It is no wonder she sent us to bed early so that she could have a bit of peace.

Vincent was 5 and started school at about this time. Joe decided that he should go to a Catholic school which was in Finchley. So, at that age he had to catch one bus up to the Great North Road, now called the A1M, get off and then wait for another bus to Finchley. He then had to cross the Great North Road and walk to school. He did not like school and did not do well there.

I loved chatting to Vincent while we were in bed although we would get in trouble if Ma heard us. I still remember a few of those chats. One time we decided to count to a million. We would take it in turns to count from one to ten as fast as possible and do it ten times. We added all the hundreds together. It went on for a long time but in due course we became bored with it. Another rather philosophical debate was about whether or not nothing could ever exist. The list of debates was endless and, I guess, mind improving. He also told me terrible lies. I tended to be a bit chesty and he delighted in telling me that I would soon die. Another time when I had a sore mouth which ached when opened, he told me and Ma that I had lockjaw, which is the common name for tetanus. This is a deadly illness and I was taken to casualty in Barnet Hospital. The doctor immediately told me that I did NOT have lockjaw and that I should stop pretending.[1]

---

[1] Granny's comment: A story Grandad does not tell here is that he and Vincent would also plot mischief, which included one time sticking Mary's hand in the mangle. She still has the scar to prove it!

Just before I was due to go to school, Ma had a "nervous breakdown." I still don't know what that meant for her. Joe was away in Australia so Vincent and myself were sent to stay with two of my father's aunts called Grace and Edith in Thornton le Dale. We had to make the journey by ourselves, by train. We were picked up by taxi from the station and taken to the house. The house was a very pretty cottage with a lovely garden. It was very snowy and I thought the countryside was lovely. It was the first time I saw a bull finch. I don't know what happened to Mary at that time but she was not with us. Vincent and myself loved going out and playing in the snow but we did not like Aunt Grace and Aunt Edie. They were old, ugly and not at all funny. They were never unkind to us but it felt like living in an old people's home. We were expected to be quiet and polite, not something we were used to. They were what one might call, "ever so nice old ladies". One thing I loved was the homemade strawberry jam.

We were sent back home three weeks later. And almost straight away, I had to go to start school. I remember the first days vividly. I hated it. Nobody talked to me and I cried continually. After a short time Ma decided to take me out of that school and to send me to my Grandmother's school. I had to catch two buses on the way to school and the same back, aged 5. I didn't like school but at least I felt reasonably at home there and I felt safe. I was there when King George VI died. My pet budgie died the same evening and I went off to school, very sad and in tears. In the morning assembly Grandma, or Mrs Williams as I had to call her when at school, obviously thought I was crying because of the King. She brought me to the front stage thinking I would be a good example to the other children. She asked me to explain why I was so sad. She was very disappointed when I replied, "I found Joey dead on the floor of his cage this morning."

One Christmas, Grandma gave me a children's encyclopaedia. I was never ever read to in our house and never read to myself so I was very disappointed at being given such a dull present. About a month later, Grandma organised a sale of unwanted clothes and toys etc to raise money for something or other. We children were all expected to play our part. So I presented the encyclopaedia in which was written "To dear little Tootles, with love and kisses,

Grandma." I was ordered to take it back home and read it. I just put on a bookshelf at home and then got rid of it after she died.

After two years at Grandma's school I was moved to the same Catholic school as Vincent. I hated it. There was lots of religion and prayers. The worst of all were the spelling tests. Having never bothered with reading or writing, I was, and still am, hopeless at spelling and very slow at reading. I certainly didn't want to read about god, being much more interested in plants, birds and fish. I came bottom in every spelling test and the child who came bottom had to stand on his chair for ten minutes. It was humiliating; it was awful.

But by luck, for me anyway, one very good thing happened towards the end of my first term at St Albans Catholic School. Vincent failed his 11 plus examination and therefore could not go to grammar school. Instead he was enrolled in the local Secondary Modern school, Ashmole School, in New Barnet. This meant that his lessons were very much to do with the trades such as woodworking, building, gardening and that sort of thing with much less emphasis on good writing skills, history, geography, etc. Joe was angry and felt that Vincent had the ability for grammar school and that St Alban's school had let him down. He took me out of St Albans after just one term and he sent me to Littlegrove County Primary in New Barnet. There, I was allowed to be scruffy, I played football and was selected for the school team as left back. I was really quite cheeky and misbehaved. I was often beaten with a slipper or ruler and I paid little attention to learning. However, one teacher in particular seemed to see something good in me. He told Ma that I was the only child he knew who could be first to answer mental arithmetic sums and do it while talking to the child behind. Another day, he asked the whole class "What is the capital city of Australia?" One of the clever clogs answered Sydney and everyone else agreed except me, I said Canberra. He brought me up to the front of the class and told every that he was very proud of me, not only because I was right but more so because I showed that you should say what you believe, even if everyone else disagrees with you. I felt that was a very important point, and I still do.

I must tell you about a very important part of my early life. When I was 6, or 7, years old, a couple called John and Rowena Bristow came to lodge in our house. They were an instant success. Ma was delighted with Rowena in particular, and they became great friends. Rowena helped in the house and John loved telling me interesting and funny stories, some of which were made up. He talked about Africa and the wildlife there. He taught me to play football and he often took me to Highbury to see Arsenal. He took me to ice hockey matches. He taught me about birds and encouraged me to get a budgerigar as a pet. After poor Joey died in his cage, Uncle John, as I called him, encouraged me to buy an aviary for the garden and to breed and sell budgerigars, which I did for a couple of years. The Bristows lived with us for about 2 years and then got their own flat quite nearby. They asked me to visit them every Sunday morning after church. I loved going to their flat. I would chat for an hour or so with John and then Rowena would cook the most delicious dinner. I thought they were the best dinners ever; but I was not allowed to say that in front of my mother. They seemed to be the only grown-ups that really liked me. John died many years ago. I recently wrote to Rowena and got a lovely letter back from her which I will treasure.

Chapter 6
The 11+

I explained earlier that Vincent failed the 11+ and went to the local secondary modern school and that Joe felt he should have passed. Joe decided to search for an academic school to accept him. Joe could not have sent him to an expensive Public school where the parents pay fees for the teaching and fees for boarding. He found a Grammar school that didn't charge teaching fees but might accept him. The trouble was that it was in Worcester. Joe visited the school and was impressed with the Head. He was told that if Vincent took and passed an entrance test set by the school, he could be admitted. Vincent passed the test and went off to Worcester. Joe had to pay relatively minor boarding fees but no tuition fees. Vincent found it difficult living away from home at first.

A year later, I was starting my last year at Littlegrove. I was not interested in passing the 11+. Anyway I was a grade B student and only about half the group A students got to Grammar School, so I didn't really stand any chance of passing. I didn't try to do well at school and I expected to go to Ashmole with my footie friends. Anyway, we all had to take the 11+ which just seemed like a load of trick puzzles to me. I soon forgot all about it. In due course, a letter arrived from the education department which I opened and read. It seemed to say that I had passed and so could go to Barnet Grammar. I was upset. I had to go off with the swots rather the footballers. I cried and protested but all to no avail. And worse was to come. Instead of going to Barnet Grammar I was going to be sent off to Worcester. The only good thing about it was that I was going to be with Vincent, and that was not particularly good.

(Paradoxically, I was writing the above paragraph when I was interrupted by Granny to see on a screen Max reading his ballet results, such a contrast.)

So, Vincent and I grumpily set off for Worcester. I knew why Vincent had to go to Worcester but I saw no good reason why I had to do the same. After all, even at Barnet Grammar, I could play football. I will later discuss why I think I was sent away but I had no idea at the time.

Anyway, I entered the school and was shown my bed in a small dormitory and the next day started in class 1A. I rather liked the dormitory and the 5 other boys seemed OK. There were no girls at the school, thank goodness. I was impressed by the school's name, Worcester Royal Grammar School. The food was fine and the school buildings and the town were really very nice. I was pleased that sport was important to the school and although we did not play football, we played rugby instead. That was OK. There were 60 boarders from all over, and about 600 dayboys who came from Worcester and the surrounding towns. Children were allocated to houses for the purposes of sport. My house was called Whiteladies and consisted of all the boarders and no one else.

Lessons did not interest me. I hated music and religious studies. Vincent told me that because I was a Catholic, I could be excused morning prayers and Protestant worship, but only as long as I went to the Catholic church every Sunday. That was a good deal!

I met and became friends with other boys and with one boarder, in particular, who loved and was good at sport and who was equally lazy about lessons. His name was Pete Downs. Pete and I mucked around in class and became the dunces of the year. That carried on until the end of the first term in the third year. By then, we were both in class 3C. Pete excelled at rugby and cricket. However, his father was angry that the school were not making him do his studies. Pete was put "on report" which meant he had to show all his homework to our housemaster before presenting it to his class teacher. If the housemaster did not judge it to be sufficiently good, he was sent back to the study room to repeat it, and given additional work to do. Pete's grades rapidly improved and he was soon near the top of the class.

That really annoyed me. I told Pete he had become a swot. He took no notice of me. That annoyed me even more. I was envious of Pete's sporting ability and I was becoming envious that he was now being told he was clever. I began to concentrate on schoolwork, secretly at first, perhaps out of jealousy or perhaps even spite. My grades improved and in the exams at the end of year I came top in some subjects. Next year, Pete was put into 4A and I was put in 4B.

I continued to do well and the following year I went into 5A with Pete for my GCE year. We both did well and both went into the 6th form to do sciences. Both of us did well in our A levels. I got the Worcester County and City Prize for the best chemistry A and S level result in Worcestershire. I never ever received a prize from the School for any academic work. The Headmaster's report said I over-achieved in exams, which I think means he thought I did better than I should have done; his last words to me were that I should respect the opinion of my betters. Pete went off to Birmingham University to study engineering. I went to Cambridge to study medicine.

Pete ended school as head prefect, captain of cricket and captain of rugby. I was appointed prefect i/c of the baths and toilets, really! Pete had a trial to play rugby for England schoolboys.

We remained friends throughout our school years but have not kept in touch since.

When I look back, I am very glad that I did not go to Barnet Grammar. It is a good school but I would not have achieved what I have done with the discipline at home. Worcester completely changed the direction of my life and I am very pleased it did so. But I still feel a little ambivalent towards Worcester. It is hard to describe it but I can tell you a true story I was told that has some affinity.

I was taking a medical history from a woman in Worksop. I don't remember the problem with the child. But I do remember what she told me. She said that about a year ago she got in trouble with the police and was sent to prison. Her child was put into care. It had taken some time before the social services allowed the child to return to her. I said I was sorry she went to prison. "No, no", she said, "It was the best thing that ever happened to me. It changed my life for the better."

Chapter 7
Cambridge

I went to Gonville and Caius College. This was the 4th largest college in Cambridge and the 4th oldest. It takes students for all types of studies just like the other 21 colleges of the university but is particularly renowned for medical studies. I believe 22 Nobel prizes have been awarded to people at Caius. In my day, most of the students came from public school rather than grammar schools. All the students were men. There were about 300 undergraduates and about 50 graduates. Most students were commoners which means an ordinary student. Exhibitioners were students who had done well in the entrance exams or in the university exams and scholars were the top 10% or so of students. I entered as a commoner.

I settled in quickly and made friends with the other 15 medics in my year. I attended lectures and tutorials. A tutorial in those days was a meeting of 2 or 3 students with one of the teachers. The teacher would go over whatever had cropped up in the recent lecture and he would ask us to write essays on the subjects in discussion. We got to know these teachers very well. There were also senior college members whose job was to keep a more general eye on the students. Each student was allocated to a tutor. A tutor is a senior college member of academic staff whose job as a tutor is to provide pastoral care to his allocated students. There was also a college director of studies who specifically looked after students of a given discipline, for instance all the medics.

We had formal examinations at the end of each academic year. Exams are graded in universities as firsts or seconds or thirds or fails. I got a first in my first and second year exams, and an upper second in my third. I was studying the principles of medical care, but not seeing patients. At the start of the second year I asked if I could study psychology as an extra subject in addition to the medical studies. My tutor agreed. So I took on nearly twice as much as the other students.

At the beginning of the second year, two of my best mates, Richard and Nick, asked me if I would join them in organising a medical expedition. I agreed but this meant I was taking on a great deal more work again, because I had to collect money from anyone who I thought might cough up. I also had to help in servicing and fitting out two land rovers. I will describe our medical expedition to Ethiopia in a later chapter. At the end of my third year I went to India to learn to treat patients in a hospital. I shall describe this later.

Caius was not all about exams and hard work. It was a great bunch of friends who had fun together. Cambridge is a lovely city and we had a smashing time together. I still meet up with those friends every few years to chat about whatever we like.

I often hear people telling school leavers not to apply to Oxford or Cambridge because it puts too much pressure on them. I disagree completely. If you want to go to the best universities in the world give it a try. Study conscientiously at school which will help you no matter what university you end up at. If you apply to Oxbridge, you will be asked to attend an interview. Just listen to the question and try to answer exactly what you believe as clearly as can. If you don't get offered a place you can still go to another university.

People also say it's for posh people. Well, nobody has ever said I am posh. I never felt other students looked down on me because I came from a non-paying school.

College life is great fun. The teaching is terrific. I made my best friendships there. There is plenty of spare time to do as you wish. The sporting and cultural facilities are excellent. The staff are very pleasant and helpful. Everyone tries to help you to do well. I think it was the nicest time of my life, at least until I married.

Chapter 8
My first love

I first met Gill at a party in our house in Blackfield in the New Forest, at a party which had been arranged by Mary for her college mates. Gill was at college with Mary where both were training to be teachers. Gill was training to be a modern dance teacher in the style of the renowned Isadora Duncan.

During the party, somebody lifted Gill up and managed to bash her head on the door lintel. She was knocked unconscious. I was called because I was a medical student, albeit at that time, never having taken any decisions about real people.

My first sight of Gill was seeing her lying on a bed; she was awake. I sat by her on the side of the bed and asked what had happened. I wanted to see if she was confused but she seemed fine. She really appreciated my efforts. She looked at me with loving eyes and I was captured. Did you know that you can tell the difference between a loving smile and a polite smile only if you look into the other's eyes? A smiling mouth without smiling eyes just signifies politeness. I asked her for a date and she agreed. The trouble was that I was in Cambridge and she was miles away in Hampshire and I had to return on Sunday. We met on Sunday morning and had a lovely time. It confirmed my love for her but I had to set off back that afternoon.

I was in a complete tizz. I could not study and my work went to pot. I took quite a while to settle down. I often went down to Hampshire to meet her and in due course my instability abated. She was a sweet kind caring person and I loved her dearly.

I invited Gill to the Caius May Ball on my last day as an undergraduate. It was wonderful and I will describe it in some detail.

It started about 9 in the evening and went on till dawn. Everyone dressed up for the evening, the men in DJs, but the girls were much more informal. They dressed in a whole array of beautiful dresses and costumes. Food and drinks of all sorts were freely available in different venues around the college. There were several bands playing different kinds of music. Gill and I particularly enjoyed a steel band. I had never even heard of a steel band before that evening. Gill was an excellent dancer and people cheered her on as she pranced about all over the lawn. That, at least, took the focus off my dancing. And, of course, we chose to eat from the West Indian barbeque. Everybody just joined in and had fun together. We stayed well into the morning, perhaps till 2 o'clock; the brave few stayed till dawn.

People often denigrate the May Balls as posh. But they are not posh. In many ways, it is a very informal affair. I don't think there was much, or even any, formal ball room dancing but if there was it did not impinge on me; I didn't see any. People just did what they wanted to do. It's just young people like Gill and myself having fun together. Young people did not drink a lot in those days. If you look on google images you will just see crowds of ordinary looking young people having fun and it was a great way to finish off my undergraduate days.

I carried on seeing Gill for another 3 years, until I qualified as a doctor, but then I was just too busy and decided to tell her that we had to finish our relationship. She was disappointed but accepted it. I still see her from time to time at Mary's house parties. She is married with 4 girls. Every time I see her I look into her smiling eyes and realise I will continue to love her for the rest of my life.

Chapter 9
University College Hospital Medical School

Towards the end of my final year at Caius I attended an interview at UCHMS. In my day Cambridge hospital was too small to train clinical medical students; there were just not enough patients. So we all had to apply to other medical schools to do our training at examining and treating patients. I was advised that UCH was the best hospital in the country, so I applied. I was interviewed and offered a place.

All the people who were accepted by UCH were invited to sit an examination for the Goldsmid Scholarship. The prize was a shield and a large sum of money. I was pleased to give it a go and I won the prize. I was awarded enough money to rent a posh flat just off Baker Street with my mate Richard.

UCH was excellent. I was there for 3 years. For the first year, I had 6 months of general medicine and in the second 6 months all types of surgery. I was not in charge of the patients. I used to see those allocated to me when they came in, clerk them in (i.e. take a full history, perform a full examination, suggest a diagnosis, suggest appropriate tests and treatments) and then report my findings and recommendations to the junior medical staff who took the first line decisions. They would question me and at times disagree with what I had decided. The consultant was always on hand as he/she had other duties as well. The consultant would do a ward round twice a week. I was expected to know all about my patients and be able to present their symptoms and findings and my conclusions, to the consultant, the junior doctors and the other medical students in my team. I would attend outpatients with the consultant who would sometimes ask me to clerk one of the patients myself and then present my finding to him. I saw hundreds of patients and I also stayed well into the evening helping out in casualty. The second and third years were much the same except that we went through the "minor" specialties, such as obstetrics and gynaecology, paediatrics, psychiatry, eyes and the pathology department. I used to go to the autopsy room every day to watch the dissection of the dead.

In the last year we were all given a 3 months elective to explore whatever field of medicine we chose. I chose to go to New Guinea.

UCH was brilliant. But it was not nearly as much fun as Cambridge. That was mainly because we all lived in separate flats and digs so we did not mix with each other nearly as much as had done at Caius. But I got a really great grounding in clinical medicine from many of the very best clinicians in the UK.

Chapter 10
Three expeditions

I made 3 expeditions during my 6 years training to be a doctor.

Ethiopia

The first was the expedition to Ethiopia. My friends, Nick Read and Richard Greenwood approached me and asked if I would care to join them in planning a medical expedition to an underdeveloped country. They were initially thinking of Guatemala in central America or the Mato Grosso in Brazil but we finally chose Ethiopia. The Dean of the medical school in Addis Ababa invited us to take on a research project about a disease called bilharzia. This would entail visiting the villages around the Great Lakes in the Rift Valley. It would involve collecting and identifying snails in the waters by the shores of the lakes and collecting samples of urine and poo from the surrounding village people.

Bilharzia is a chronic (i.e. long standing) debilitating disease caused by a worm that lives in the blood vessels around the bladder and lower gut. It is caught by wading in water that contains an embryo worm. The embryo grows in certain types of snail.

I need to describe to you how this worm starts and finishes it life. This is called a life cycle, because the life starts as an egg and finishes with the worm laying an egg. This cycle is repeated over and over again ad infinitum. You can start the cycle any place you want but let's start the cycle as an egg. Stage 1, the eggs are laid by an adult female worm in the tissues around the bowel and bladder and some pass into the stool and urine. If urine or stool is passed into or leaks into a lake we enter stage 2. Stage 2, the eggs hatch and release the first stage larvae into the waters of the lake. These first stage larvae search out appropriate snails. Stage 3, the larvae bite their way into the snail and grow there by eating away at the snail's body. The snail dies and releases these fattened up second stage larvae into the waters of the lake. Stage 4, the second stage larvae search out an appropriate human to feed on. When they find skin of a human wading in the water, they gnaw their way through the skin and invade a small vein. They flow with the blood to the heart and lungs and then round the circulation to the small arteries of the bowel or bladder. There they mature into adult worms, mate and lay their eggs, thereby setting up stage 1 again. This cycle is repeated over and over again. The adult worms in the walls of the bladder and bowel damage these tissues and cause bleeding. This is the illness called bilharzia.

Our job was to collect poos and wees from the villagers to see if they were passing eggs and to look in the waters to see if the lake contained the right sort of snails for the transmission of bilharzia. We had to collect loads of money to buy two land rovers so that we could drive to and from Ethiopia and then to and around the lakes. We had to buy tickets for the ship from Marseilles to Djibouti both for us and for the land rovers. We had to buy tents. I had to write about 200 letters asking for money. I was often asked to go to company headquarters in London to explain what we were going to do, and why I needed the money, and to ask for a contribution of money. It was also my job to help our mechanic to service and maintain the land rovers.

Three more students joined our team one of whom was the head mechanic.

We set off after the May Ball at the end of our last summer term. We drove down to the south coast and got a plane across the channel. We then drove all the way down France to Marseilles. We slept there in a railway shunting yard close to the docks and the next morning we boarded the SS Ferdinand de Lessops for a 10-day trip to Djibouti. We travelled 4th class which meant we slept in a dark, below deck hold crammed in with French soldiers. The food was dreadful but we were allowed on deck. We met an English girl called Sarah Stone and she joined our group. We sailed across the Mediterranean, close to an active volcano called Stromboli, and on to Port Said in Egypt to enter the Suez Canal. Then south down the Red Sea to Djibouti.

We disembarked at Djibouti in French Somaliland and boarded a train to Dire Dawa. We crossed the great Danakil Depression which is the hottest place on earth. The Danakil tribe is the most feared in Africa. Their reputation is that if they fight you and win they will chop off your willy and then wear it round their neck as a trophy. I bought the dagger I keep in the dining room from a Danakil tribesman but he seemed friendly enough to me. I decided not to fight him! We were protected on this journey by soldiers from the French Foreign Legion.

We arrived in Dire Dawa the next day and then set off to Addis Ababa in the land rovers. Sarah invited us to stay in the house that she rented while we sorted exactly what we were meant to do. We then set off to do our job.

The first site was the Awash River. We set our tents on a lovely grassy slope down to the river and had our first camp meal. It all felt grand but in the middle of the night there was a storm and we were in danger of having our things washed down into the river. We quickly brought everything up to the top of the hill, and we had learnt our first of many weaknesses.

Next day we set off to collect snails and to visit local villages.
Collecting snails was potentially dangerous because of others in the river, the crocodiles and pythons! One person would enter the river in waders with a rope around his waist, scraping the river bed with a sort of shrimping net for 2 minutes while two others just stood on the bank keeping a watch for movement in the water.

After the 2 minutes was up, the wader would pass his catch of snails to those on the bank. We were never approached by a croc but we saw a few in the water and we never took any risks. The others would be on the river bank classifying and counting the snails and mapping the site. We would then move 100 paces up the river and repeat the exercise. On one occasion, one of my colleagues trod on a hidden python which was lying in the reeds by the side of the river and they both leaped with surprise and ran off in opposite directions.

Collecting samples of poo and wee from the villagers was much more fun. We would go into the village and ask to speak to the head man to gain his permission to collect the samples. We paid for the samples with cigarettes, two for a poo and one for a wee. I remember that their word for a wee is a shinte, rather like a rude word for a poo in English. The villagers found us very funny and asked us many questions. They found it very funny that we wanted to buy poos and wees and were always asking what we wanted it for. They asked us if we liked their young women and if we would buy one as a wife. They asked us if we had sisters and how many cows our sisters would cost. They always wanted a nice fat wife, not a skinny little one.

We saw lots of wild animals and bird. Hyenas, wild boar, baboons and colobus monkeys were common, as were fish eagles, pelicans, flamingos and marabou storks.

After we had visited all the sites and done our job we returned to Addis with our samples. I spent hours every day for a week looking down a microscope at samples of poo and wee. We did not find much evidence of bilharzia and the lakes of the Rift Valley have now been opened for tourists.

The Rift Valley is a wonderful sight. As you drive up towards it you suddenly see this huge wide valley in front of you which goes on right into the distance and looks as if it is half a mile deep. At first sight, it looks as if it would be impossible to drive down such a precipitous slope. But they have cut a zig zag path all the way down. It takes ages to do it and it is a bit scary. Geologists say that it will split the African continent in two and end up as a sea between the two parts of Africa. Just as continents can drift together to push up mountains, so they can drift apart and create rift valleys and then oceans. In fact, the Danakil desert that we crossed in the train is the top part of the rift valley and is already below sea level. Sea water drains into the depression from the Red Sea, but it is so hot there that it continually evaporates away, leaving huge salt deposits.

The Ethiopia trip was my first experience of going abroad. I loved it and I loved the lads I went with. We still meet from time to time. Sarah was very frail last time I saw her. The Christmas before last she wrote a very jolly card for me and then happily went off to sleep. She died that night. I have kept her card as a treasured memory.

India

After leaving Cambridge and before starting at UCH I went to India. I had become interested in tropical medicine in Ethiopia and wanted to develop skill in that field. I wrote to a hospital in Erode and got a welcoming reply from the medical director. Erode is a large town in the State of Chenai which is in the southern part of

India. Chenai was called Madras State at that time. I flew to Mumbai, which used to be called Bombay. I was amazed at what I saw. It was a huge, overcrowded, buzzy, bustling city but I had to catch a train down to Chenai that morning so I decided to explore Mumbai on my way home.

I went to the crowded station and bought the cheapest ticket to Erode and boarded the waiting train. I had to give a “tip” to the man in the ticket office. The carriage was packed with Indians who were obviously of the poorest class. It was very hot. There was a strong smell of spices and of sweat. I liked the smell of spices but I had never tasted a curry because at that time there were no curry restaurants in England (also, nobody in England knew what a pizza was at that time).

The train set off. It slowly chugged through Mumbai on a narrow rail track overlooked by blocks of flats with washing hanging out of many of the windows to dry. Men and women stood looking out from the balconies but seemed totally uninterested in the passing train.

Before long we got into the countryside. We passed small villages. The houses were really huts. The women and children were mostly bare footed. The roads were dirt tracks and goats and cows roamed here and there. The cows were large and white with enormous horns. They seemed friendly. People were carrying buckets of something. I guessed water from the well. The women often carried food baskets on their heads and sometimes massive loads of firewood on their backs. It was so different from England and life seemed so simple and peaceful.

We stopped at several stations. They were busy bustling affairs. Lots of people got off at the station and I noticed that many were buying food and drink from the sellers and then rejoining the train. Others were leaving the train and even more were boarding at the station.

The people on the train were interested in me and many were friendly. They warned me about thieves on the train and told me they would look after me. But of course, I was worried that they may have been the thieves, just trying to get control of me. But nobody did me any harm.

It was a two-day trip with one night in between. I had booked the cheapest ticket. The carriage had rows of slatted wood plank benches with the three benched positioned one on top of the other like a three shelved book case. It was called a three-tier carriage but they pronounced it "three tire" I was advised to grab a bench well before evening or else I might have to stand all night. At the next station I got out of the train and bought a cup of chai and some strange looking snacks. The chai was tea made with condensed milk and a bucket load of sugar; it was delicious. I had never seen anything like the snacks. But they were absolutely delicious. I immediately loved Indian food.

After eating, I grabbed my sailors' duffel bag and climbed onto a top tier bunk. I had been advised to get a top plank because "fluids" often dripped through to the lower planks. I cuddled my bag against my belly and chest and began to think of going to sleep. But it was uncomfortable. The wooden benches were hard and there weren't any pillows. I had no option. To make matters worse an old chap climbed up to my bench and joined me. He snored all night. I dozed off from time to time.

I came down from my site early in the morning so that I could stand by the big open windows and watch India waking up. I got off at the stations to buy chai and to try all the different snacks. Before too long we were chugging into Erode.

The hospital was called The Church of South India Christian Missionary Hospital. Its head was a middle-aged man called David and his wife. They said I should live with them in their smallish but otherwise typical Indian bungalow. (The word bungalow comes from India and the meaning is not quite the same as in England; use google images to see Indian bungalows.) They were a delightful couple, interesting knowledgeable and in every way helpful. We had lovely meals each day cooked by an Indian lady. I was put to work in the hospital straight away. The hospital served the poorest people in Erode. I sat with the doctors in their busy outpatients and quickly learned how to examine and treat patients. Remember that at that stage I had not yet worked in a hospital in England. I went on ward rounds and learnt how to treat very sick people. I saw lots of patients with tropical diseases. I learned to diagnose and treat conditions like typhoid, leprosy, TB, malnutrition, malaria, worms and lots of others. I learnt to give chloroform anaesthetics. Unfortunately, one patient died of an anaesthetic related complication when I was the anaesthetist which a more experienced anaesthetist would have managed better than me. All the doctors were delightful and helpful but my favourite was a beautiful young lady called Raja Lukshmi. She and the others invited me out to eat in an ordinary Indian restaurant with them shortly before I set off home to England. It was a lovely evening. She gave me the lovely little cobra oil lamp which is in our bedroom in Worksop.

One day David and his wife invited me on a trip with them to pick tea in the Nilgiri Hills. These hills are blanketed with fields of tea plants, with ladies in colourful saris and large bags over their shoulder into which they threw the young tea shoots. A tea bush is a camelia which comes from China as opposed to the flowering camelia one sees in the UK which originated in Japan. I buy Nilgiri tea whenever I go to Lincoln just to remember India. We had tea at the home one of their friends. David and his wife commented on how lovely her apostle tea spoons were and his wife said she was so envious.

In due course I returned home. I was an expert by then in travelling three tier class. I stayed in Bombay for a week in the YMCA. I explored the city. I searched for and found an apostle spoon which I sent to David and his wife as a thank you. I saw many begging lepers in the streets. I saw huge manta ray leaping out of the ocean at the great Gateway of India and I was sad to leave such a lovely country and people behind.

The Fore Valley

Shortly before the final medical exams, students were given 3 months off to revise or in some other way pursue their medical interests. I had read a medical report about a newly discovered condition, called kuru, by an Australian called David Matthews. Kuru was found in only one remote valley in the Eastern Highlands of New Guinea. The tribe were cannibals, eating their dead relatives and this was thought perhaps to be the cause. Kuru was a lethal brain disease affecting mainly the cerebellum and therefore balance.

I immediately thought that I could spend my three months in the Fore Valley. I wrote to David asking if I could help with the research. In due course I received a letter from the head of the Australian Institute of Human Biology saying that they would welcome me and offering me a grant from the Australian Medical research council to fund the trip. New Guinea was an Australian Protectorate at this time.

I flew to Port Moresby in New Guinea and from there in a small aeroplane to Goroko in the Eastern Highlands. The aeroplane could not fly over the highest mountains and so flew up the river valleys. Naked children from the higher slopes waved down to us as we flew past. I could see out of the pilot's front window. From time to time the plane seemed to be heading straight into mountain side ahead, only for the pilot to make a sharp turn into another valley. The aerodrome in Goroka was just a long grass field with a few huts and hangers.

The Institute had a small office in Goroko. I was taken by land rover from Goroka to Okapa in the Fore Valley. We travelled a good road going east/west down the spine of the Highlands and then went off road down tracks to Okapa. Okapa was a small native village with one wooden hut belonging to the Institute. I found another newly arrived British medical student called David Moir from Oxford already ensconced there and awaiting my arrival. He was much earlier in his medical training than me and not used to examining patients, while I had completed my three-year training in clinical medicine at UCH. He had already decided our schedule; he should be the organiser and I should do the clinical work This suited me.

The schedule was that we should spend 5 consecutive days walking from one village to another examining all the patients in each village. He had organised some provisions and equipment and a native interpreter who could speak some English, as well as the Fore language, and our guides.

The New Guinea Highlands are indeed highlands. The treks from one village to the next were arduous. The mountains are very high and the slopes precipitous. We were at high altitude, somewhere near 8000 ft. There were only very poorly marked tracks. At higher levels the way was clearer, because one could see into the distance, but on the lower slopes we were often scrambling through dense jungle.[2]

When we arrived in a village, the interpreter and the guides would introduce us to the chief and ask his permission to see any people who had kuru. Kuru was their name for this illness. Kuru means "kranky" walking in the Fore language. Kranky is a lovely Australian word for broken but still working. We would usually see one, two or three patients. Some would be young children.

[2] Comment from Granny: Grandad told me how it was so difficult that one day he was so exhausted that he told the guides to just leave him on the side of the mountain as he could go no further. They didn't, of course.

The diagnosis was simple. Even in the early stages these patients could not walk in a straight line. They walked like a very drunken person. Diagnosis was essentially made by using the same test that police used when I was young to decide if someone was too drunk to drive; "Just walk along this straight line, please, Sir." I did a formal assessment of the severity which required more skill. The patients all died within 3 years and the patient and all the villagers knew it.

We were told a lot about black magic which was always attributed as the cause of unexpected and unexplained adverse events. When we were walking between villages we would often chew sugar cane sticks which the villagers gave us to use both as food and as walking sticks. The guides made me spit out the inedible part of the canes into a bag which they buried. They said if anyone found the remains of my canes they could do black magic on me whenever they chose. I had to obey. When in Rome, do as the Romans do.

A Japanese neurologist wrote to ask if he could come and see some kuru patients because he thought it might give him clues to the cause of motor neurone disease. We agreed and showed him some cases.

He invited me to visit his hospital in Wakayama on my way home and said I would be enrolled on his staff roll as assistant professor in neurology so that he could fund my expenses. I was delighted to agree. It was very different and interesting. I visited the Great Exhibition 1970 in Osaka and I travelled to Tokyo on the bullet train to board my plane back home. And I was a professor of medicine even before I had qualified!

Two of the doctors who worked on kuru were awarded the Nobel Prize. It was discovered that the well-known condition, Creutzveld Jacob Disease, was the same condition as naturally occurring kuru. Later the UK had the terrible variant CJD syndrome and the mad cow disease scandal; all just kuru manufactured by the farming industry when they decided to feed the vegetarian cows with offal.

Chapter 11
Dr Williams, the beginnings and his second love

I've just passed my finals.

I had had a lovely case in the all-important finals oral examination. I was asked to discuss a young girl who had recently been in south Spain and after coming home she developed fever, diarrhoea and the doctor noticed a pink spot on her belly. I immediately guessed it was typhoid because I had seen about 200 cases in India but I decided to play it canny. The Prof asked me to suggest a diagnosis. I said it could have been any one of several possibilities but by far the most likely was typhoid: rose coloured spots on the abdomen are an important diagnostic point. I was right, of course and I passed my finals.

By a huge stroke of luck, several years later, in my oral examination to become a specialist, I was posed with a similar question. I answered promptly that it could be typhoid. "Very good", said the examiner, and then "Have you ever seen a case?" "Yes", I replied, "there was a suspected case a bit like that in the children's ward in UCH and I kept an eye on her investigations. She proved to be positive for typhoid. "Do you know anything about typhoid I was asked?" "Yes a little", I replied, "I thought it was something I ought to know about so I read it up." "Well, tell me what you know.", he replied, and I knew I would know much more than he did. He stopped me after a while but by then I knew I had passed by the approving looks on his face. It's good to take control of your examiner!

I worked at two hospitals in the first year after qualifying as a junior house officer. This is the most junior level of doctor and is seen very much as a training post. The first job was in UCH. I was the junior to a mixed post of general medicine, neurology and rheumatology. The boss of the general medical firm was Lord Rosenheim, a brilliant physician and President of the Royal College of Physicians. I did not see very much of him but the junior consultant was John Stokes, almost as famous in the upper echelons of medicine, being a vice-president of the College. It was a great starting job except that the registrar rarely appeared and I was on my own rather a lot and had to take more important decisions than other juniors.

The second job was in Portsmouth. I was house surgeon to the senior surgical consultant whose main field was abdominal surgery and to the cancer unit where I would help to organise the radiotherapy and administer the cancer drugs. We had a jolly good registrar. Both jobs were very good and I had an excellent introduction to clinical medicine.

I next moved to Stoke on Trent, determined to pursue a career in general medicine. For me, Stoke was the best hospital possible. I was there for 16 months and I rotated to different specialties every 4 months. I worked under consultants for general medicine, endocrinology, neurology, cardiology, respiratory diseases, dermatology and rheumatology. You couldn't have better experience, and there were teaching rounds several times a week for about only 6 young trainees. I thrived on it. I passed my specialist examinations and decided I needed to move on to the big London Hospitals. The bosses wanted me to stay on in Stoke and told me I would continue to get better training in Stoke than I would in London. But I knew better, and applied and was appointed to the post of medical registrar to the professorial unit at the Westminster Hospital. But, boy how things were going to change for the worse.

I started on 1st January 1973. I was surprised how few patients came to the hospital. There was a great deal of teaching but little practical work to do. I hoped it would improve. Towards the end of the month three girl medical students came to sit with me at the lunch table. They told me that they particularly enjoyed my teaching. They told me that their friend Sue was returning from her elective in Canada and she too would love my teaching. They shared a flat with Sue. They asked me if I had a girl friend and I replied that I hadn't.

On Monday morning I had to take the teaching round for the medical students. I asked an elderly lady if I could teach about her rare condition. She replied yes, saying she always enjoyed the students because they seemed such nice young people. The 6 students arrived on time and there was a new face. She was beautiful and listened carefully to the questions I posed to the group and listened to their responses. I had given a lot of information that was pointing to the diagnosis but no one seemed to have put it all together to make a diagnosis, and nor did I expect them to, as it was an unusually rare condition and I had planned to use the lady to demonstrate the principles of assessing anaemia, not as a diagnostic quiz. I asked the new-comer if she had any ideas or comments she would like to make. She replied in a confident voice, "I think it all points to hereditary haemorrhagic telangectasis and I say that because of the tiny red spots on Mrs Whatever's lips". She was right. I was impressed. The other students looked as if they had not even heard of this condition. I asked Sue to describe the condition and to explain how she had come to the diagnosis. I listened to her clear excellent analysis and thought how impressive she was.

I phoned her that evening and asked if we could meet for dinner the next evening. She agreed.

We met after work outside her flat and walked to a restaurant on the boating lake in Hyde Park. As we sat eating at the table, I couldn't take my eyes off her long black hair which she was allowing to fall provocatively across her face. I wanted to brush it back but I did not dare. She rested her hands on the table while chatting. I touched her hands but didn't dare hold them. We slowly walked back to her flat bumping each other's shoulders as we walked. At the entrance I asked her if I could kiss her and if we could meet again. We continued to see each other in all our spare time and almost every day. I was smitten and I think she was.

But I was becoming increasingly disappointed with the Westminster Hospital and in particular with one of the consultants that I had to work with. In mid-February I tendered my resignation but the consultant said he wanted me to rescind the resignation and that things would improve. I agreed to his request because I was enjoying my relationship with Sue, but unfortunately nothing did improve.

I knew that if I resigned, I would have difficulty in getting another registrar post and my consultant told me he would not support me unless I stayed in post. The situation at the Westminster was getting worse, so I finally did resign and left. I thought I would not be able to progress further in my aim to be a consultant physician without a supportive reference from him. I decided that I would have to enter general practice. I decided to start my GP training with paediatrics. I applied for a job caring for new-born babies in Slough. I was offered the post as a junior house officer and I accepted. It was a short post for only two and a half months, I imagine filling in for an absent junior. I was fascinated at treating these tiny babies. I applied myself at the job and was doing well.

Sue qualified and started her post in the Westminster at about the same time as I was started at Slough. We both had demanding jobs but we spent much of our spare time together. Everything seemed to me to be going well with our relationship. I would have liked to discuss our future together but she would never be drawn into that conversation. She did suggest I might like to buy a cottage in the Cotswolds, going half and half with her, but I declined because she had not considered any future together.

My job in Slough was coming towards the end. The consultant asked me if I would like to take the junior children's ward post at the sister hospital in Wexham Park. I was delighted and accepted.

About this time, Sue told me that she was going on holiday with friends for two weeks in the Alps. We had been on holiday twice together before this and I asked if I could come. She very firmly said, "No." I felt a strong foreboding that this would mark the end of our relationship, but I desperately hoped not.

Two weeks later she called me at Wexham Park saying she wanted to come over to speak to me. She told me our relationship was over. She did not give any explanation but she said I must never ever contact her again. And then she left. I cried for the rest of the evening. Next morning, I resolved just to get on with life. I did write to her a couple of years ago. I explained how lucky I have been in life with a super family and a successful career. She wrote back promptly, described her career and family life. She mentioned that she got married in September 1974, about 10 months after she went on that holiday; I guess he was one of her friends. She has had a good life but she was widowed in 2015 when she would have been 66 or 67; poor thing, just the thing I am not looking forward to for either Granny or me. I don't think I will ever write to her again but I still think of her from time to time.

Wexham Park was even better than Slough. In particular, I enjoyed the interaction with children and their mothers. It was eye-opening to see how hard the mothers tried to help the children while we were doing horrible things like sticking needles in them. I was impressed and wondered if Ma would have done the same for me. And the children seemed to like me, they seemed to think I was funny. The job went very well. The boss knew that I wanted to go through the specialties so that I could be a well-rounded GP. He advised that I take the junior obstetrics job in another sister hospital in Ascot. I took his advice.

However, Wexham Park had changed my vision of my future. I realised that I could progress in hospital medicine if I were to choose to do so and I could become a GP if I so wished. I decided to develop my range of skills even further by going abroad.

Heatherwood Hospital is just opposite the Ascot racecourse. I started in about April 1974. I was working for a remarkably wise obstetrician called Stan Simmons. Stan recognised that I would never make an obstetrician; I did not like operating or using forceps. He knew I liked the babies and that I was well versed in many fields of medicine. He encouraged me to study the endocrinology of women's hormones and, when he heard that I had done hundreds of lumber punctures, he encouraged me to introduce an epidural service into the obstetric department. We became the second hospital in the UK to have an epidural service. I was fascinated about how women go into labour and we talked about it together.

We had no real notion about how labour starts then, but it has been since then my life-long ambition to discover what makes the uterus change from a stable closed organ to an open active organ discharging its contents. And I think I have discovered what starts labour, but the trouble is that only a few endocrinologists agree with me. No obstetricians do.

While I was working in Ascot, I applied for a general duties job in Zambia and was accepted. But my real weakness at the Ascot job was that I did not like doing surgery and had shown no skill in it. I decide to apply for an anaesthetic post so that I could assist the surgeons by anaesthetising the patients rather than doing the surgery.

I was appointed to a 3-months anaesthetics post in Bromley, Kent. I found anaesthetics boring but I had no difficulty learning the practice of anaesthetics.

I went off to Zambia pretty uncertain what my future would hold for me but determined to enjoy myself.

Chapter 12
Chililabombwe, Zambia

I was driven from Ndola airport to the NCCM mine hospital in the town of Chililabombwe. I was shown round the hospital by the medical director and introduced to each ward and to the medical and nursing staff. The junior medical staff were all British and seemed a good mix of nice men and women. They were delightfully informal. One bloke said to me, "We've heard all about you. You sound awful", but he and the others were laughing and smiling. I knew I would fit in and that we would get on OK. I was taken to my flat. It was a nice small flat with passion fruits growing at the back and an avocado tree; it suited me, jolly well.

I was asked to report for duty early next morning and immediately sent to my first outpatient session. There was a colleague there and we had to work through all the waiting patients. I was told to be quick because we might have to see more than 100 patients; we had to see whoever turned up. I was assisted by an interpreter. All the patients were Africans, because the ex-pats were seen in a different clinic by the boss. Most of the patients had minor complaints and came because they needed off-work certificates. A typical minor consultation might go; "What's the matter?", "I've got a bad cough.", "Then cough, please?". I would listen and look and then decide if it was nothing, a minor chest infection or a bad infection. I would only examine if I thought it was bad. Most were sorted out in a minute or two. We made mistakes and some patients returned and were re-evaluated more carefully. The patients knew the system and worked it well. There were some serious cases. There was a lot of malaria and TB and quite a lot of venereal disease, and of nasty injuries. There were women and children to be seen as well. They tended to be more ill because none of them were coming just to get off–work certificates.

I got used to seeing a lot of patients quickly and understood that it was the only way we could run the hospital for the most benefit to the population.

I was allocated to take charge of the adult medical ward and told I would swap to other wards from time to time. My next ward was the maternity ward and care of the sick new-borns. It was agreed that I would not do any surgery. It was perfect training for a prospective general practitioner in England. We were called in at night to see very sick patients or to do operations. I would always give the anaesthetic.

I gave epidurals to some of the women in the maternity unit. They were amazed and the women said I did this by magic. They laughed at me saying it was white magic, not like their magic!

One little baby had a bad eye infection. I gave her mother a bottle of eye drops and told her to put one drop into each eye each time she fed the baby. She came back the next day asking for another bottle. I said, "You can't have used up a whole bottle in 24 hours." The nurse said to me, "African mothers are not like English mothers. We feed our babies whenever they cry but your mothers only do it every 4 hours. I learned the lesson.

Here is another story you might like. A lot of babies and toddlers were admitted because of severe malnutrition. Malnutrition with measles was common and was very dangerous. Many of these babies died. Malnutrition and chicken pox were also common but not quite so serious. Chicken pox is itchy. The nurses used to paint the skin with calamine lotion which dries to a peach/pink powder on the skin. African babies usually have protuberant belly buttons. Everybody loved the sight of the little toddlers playing together and toddling around, half of them peach coloured and the other half black. They looked like two football teams of pot-bellied dwarfs.

The boss, who was the consultant physician, looked after the ex-pat medical cases. He retired about 4 months after I had started. Another senior doctor was appointed but he became the general manager and did not do any clinical work. He came to me and asked if I would take the place of the consultant physician. I agreed on condition that I could take over the children's care as well as the adults. He agreed, of course.

I moved from Chililabombwe to a bigger hospital in Chingola. I was given a posher house and a bigger car because I needed to travel between the hospitals. I had two big medical wards, a TB ward and the children's ward to look after in Chingola, and in Chililabombwe a paediatric and an adult's ward; about 200 beds in all. I also had to look after the ex-pats in both hospitals. It was busy but I did not have to work through the nights, which was nice. The work was much the same as before with few exceptions. I was responsible for many more inpatients and therefore unexpected and rare difficult situations arose more often. I had nobody to ask for advice, so I just had to do my best. I learned a lot about the treatment of TB and other diseases.

A great pandemic of meningitis was sweeping across Africa at the time. We treated more than 100. We noticed that if the patients were not improving by 4 hrs after admission they would likely die. We decided that the nurses should give an injection of high dose penicillin as soon as possible after admission if they thought the patient had meningitis, and if they were very ill we would not do a lumbar puncture to check the diagnosis. The mortality rate dropped dramatically. This way of treating meningitis would have been frowned upon in the UK at the time.

I saw several young African men who became unwell with fever, weight loss, various infections and then just continued to get worse and died. I sent off all sorts of tests but never found the cause. Years later, after I returned home, I read about the discovery of AIDS and realised that that had been what I was seeing. My colleagues in Chingola found some old microscope slides from patients in my time. These slides were tested for the AIDS virus and found to be positive. Because of this, it is, or at least was, accepted that the AIDS epidemic started in the area of southern Congo and northern Zambia.

I seemed to cope quite well with all the work in Chingola. There were highs and lows.

A young man was admitted with a high fever and a swollen painful knee. I thought he had a severe infection in the knee and decided to put a needle into the joint to inject antibiotic into the knee and to give him injections of penicillin. I scrubbed and gowned and gloved up and prepared the syringe of penicillin. I pushed the needle and withdrew blood, not pus. I injected the penicillin. He was dead by the morning, having bled from the injection sites and from his mouth and rectum. It immediately struck me that his swollen knee was most likely due to a bleeding abnormality like haemophilia, and not an infection in the joint. My treatment had killed him; a very sobering lesson.

The mother of a baby taught me an even more painful lesson. The baby was called Happy. She was admitted at about 8 months of age with severe malnutrition and diarrhoea. We tried everything to make her better but she just continued to get worse and it was clear that she was going to die. I even tried to feed her through a drip. It is a procedure I had done previously in adults but not in babies. It did not work and after a few days it was even more clear that she would die. I told the mother that she should take her out to one of the veranda beds and just be nice and loving to her because she was dying. I forgot all about her. About a month later my ward round was interrupted by a nurse who told that there a lady who insisted on talking to me. I said to bring her in and I would see her after I had seen this patient. I went over to see a lady holding a bonny baby. She asked me if I knew who she was. I replied that I did not. She angrily told me that she was Happy's mother and that I had not even bothered to visit her on the veranda. She told me she was better at doctoring than I was and that I should go back to England. Since then I have always tried, even if the odds seemed hopeless, and always remained involved when it is clear a patient is going to die. I have probably had more thank-yous from the mothers of children who have died under my care than from those that have survived.

I did have successes as well. One was a little girl of about 3 who came in gasping for breath and severely pale. Her blood count showed a severe anaemia, something less than 1 gram per 100 ml; it should be about 12gram/100ml. She was dying in front of me of heart failure. I had never seen such anaemia before and never since. I decided to do an exchange transfusion. This is a procedure in which the patient's dilute blood is removed from a vein in one arm while concentrated blood is transfused into the other arm at the same time and the same rate. I had done it in new-borns but never in children. She got better quickly after three or four exchanges and started complaining about me hurting her. She pulled out one of the drips and effectively forced me to stop. From then on, all she needed was iron syrup and de-worming tablets.

Another young lady came into the ward close to death in heart failure. She had a high fever. She did not look anaemic. Her heart sound seemed unusually quiet and I could not feel her heart when I put my hand on her chest. The veins in her neck were distended.

I decided this was a condition I had never before seen, called cardiac tamponade: that is when a large amount of fluid under pressure collects in the sac in which the heart lies. The pressure of the fluid stops the blood flowing into the heart and therefore the heart cannot pump out blood. I pushed a needle through the front of her chest and was delighted to see pus pouring out. I put her on antibiotics and was delighted to see her going home in a few days.

The last patient I will describe was a young English ex-pat with high fever who told me his urine was dark brown. We tested his urine found a lot of blood and we found malaria parasites in his blood. He had severe kidney damage. This is a condition called blackwater fever, which happens when a severe infection with malaria ruptures the red cells which release free haemoglobin into the circulation. The released blood goes dark, just as it would on a handkerchief. There were no facilities in Zambia for dialysing people in renal failure but I could not get him on a flight to the UK for another week. His renal failure deteriorated over the next couple of days and he was beginning to retain too much fluid and go into heart failure. His only chance was dialysis. I decided to try. The hospital brought in lots of bottles of saline. We added potassium and glucose to these to draw water out of his circulation which would improve his heart failure. We made a cut into his belly and inserted a feeding tube. We warmed the saline bags in the basin in his room and then attached the bag to the feeding tube and poured all the fluid into his abdomen by lifting the bag on a drip stand. We left the empty bag attached to the catheter for an hour and then placed the attached bag on the floor to allow the fluid to drain out. We repeated this cycle of filling and emptying the fluid many times over the next hours until the blood test results improved. The number of cycles decreased as the malaria resolved and the heart failure came under control. He flew to Manchester a week later and sometime after that he wrote to me saying he was back home with normal kidney function. We subsequently used the same technique on several more patients with blackwater fever.

Zambia was not all about work. I played tennis with my old mate in Chililabombwe. I went off at weekends to the game parks.

One special doctor came to work in Chililabombwe who changed my life forever.

I have forgotten the name of the boss who I met on my first day in Zambia. But he had a good friend called Jack Todd, who was a consultant physician in England. They had been medical students together. Jack had a son who was early in his medical career called Peter. Peter wanted to work abroad and asked his dad to suggest a venue. Jack wrote to his friend asking if Zambia would be good experience. The boss said that there would be nowhere better than Chililabombwe.

The boss told me that were getting a new doctor called Peter Todd and that he was the son of his old friend Jack Todd. I recognised the name Jack Todd because he wrote frequent letters in the British Medical Journal criticising British medical practice. I thought the letters were very wise. The boss confirmed it was his friend who wrote those letters. I will come back to this in due course.
Peter and I became good friends and good colleagues in Chililabombwe.

I have no more to say about Zambia. It is time to return to restart my career in England.

Chapter 13
The Love of Sheffield

I was appointed registrar at Sheffield Children's Hospital in June 1976. I worked the first 6 months looking after the prem babies; it was just about OK. I then spent a year on the children's ward which was better, but no better than Wexham Park. I worked in the pathology lab with Professor Emery for the last 6 months. His specialty was cot deaths but I was not particularly interested.
I bought a flat in Sheffield.

One morning in the spring of 1977, when I was on the children's ward, I was bleeped for an outside call. The caller said that I did not know her but my friend Peter Todd was her cousin, and he was coming to visit her. She suggested we all meet up. I replied that I did not have a friend called Peter Todd. She seemed confused by this and then asked me if I had worked in Zambia; the penny dropped, it all made sense, then. "Yes, I remember, I would to meet love to meet up with him again." She told me her name was Catherine Todd.

The dinner went well. I think Granny's friend Sheila and her boyfriend Kevin were also at the dinner.[3] There were various interesting topics of debate and the good-hearted disagreements were fun. I said I was intending to arrange a house-warming party in my new flat and that I would invite Catherine and Sheila.

I didn't get on with any arranging but I often thought about Catherine. She seemed an interesting and engaging woman but I felt too unsure of myself to call her. She broke this impasse and called me, asking when the house-warming party was to take place. "Quite soon but I have not yet finalised the date." I bought a load of wine, cheese, fruit and biscuits and invited some of the doctors and Catherine. It wasn't an inspiring party. Catherine came with Sheila. We did not talk much but I plucked up courage and invited her back to my flat for dinner the following Monday after work.

---

[3] Granny's comment: Actually, Kevin wasn't there, it was just Sheila.

I made bread. I bought sirloin steak, potatoes and cabbage, a cheesecake and some wine. I boiled the steak, cabbage and potatoes in a saucepan, for 15 minutes until tender. Mine was very nice indeed, but she has never stopped complaining about hers, even yet; ungrateful woman! Anyway, we got on like a house on fire. I was captivated by her. I asked her if we could meet the next day. She declined saying she had a prior engagement. I've still not got over that! She did add that she would be happy meet the following day. I graciously agreed. Wednesday was even better and then on Thursday we discussed our ambitions about families and about children and the future. I don't remember if it was explicitly stated that the conversations were about us together. However, we agreed to spend the weekend in her house doing nothing of interest other than seeing if we could cope with each other. The implication was pretty obvious. I don't know the exact date of that weekend but it was about this time of year; end of March or early April. We have rarely been separated from each other for a whole day in the 43 years since then.

What was it that we liked about each other? I don't know. But I will think and try to answer that question for myself. Certain things are obvious. We were the right ages, we both wanted to be married and have children, we were both well established in interesting careers that overlapped to some degree, we both had the potential to do well in our careers, we liked challenging each other's opinions and could cope with the challenge, we were both left of centre in our political views, we are both for the most part happy and optimistic and free from major hang-ups. And she was a good-looking lady without the need for glamour paraphernalia. But all that is not enough to ensure a lasting relationship. It is a good basis on which to set off on the unforeseeable journey. Success comes only if both partners are comfortable and continue to find mutual benefit in their togetherness. I still find her nice, funny, a great mother and grandmother, intolerably argumentative and I enjoy being in her presence.

The weekend together went well. I think Granny read for much of the time. I remember trying to fix her housemate's car and pottering around in her tiny garden. She fed me well and we spent much of the time together. I did not feel bored and was pleased just to be with her. That sealed it for me.

The following week, we spent all our free time together and I knew we were going to get married. We arranged to go away together to Cambridge for the coming weekend. On the Saturday evening we ate in an Italian restaurant and applauded each other about what a fine pair we made. I knew what I had to do but it came out a tiny bit clumsy; "Well, we might as well get married?" She had a look of shock and joy on her face and when she had stopped laughing, replied, "Well, yeh, maybe."

We set about making arrangements. We wanted to marry as soon as possible but the earliest we could arrange it was the 3rd September. We told our parents. Audrey and Alan were delighted with the news and shortly thereafter came up to Sheffield to meet me.

Ma was less pleased. Joe just kept quiet. We arranged to go down to their house in Brockenhurst. The weekend was an unpleasant disaster. Ma had decided that she did not like Granny because she was a Protestant, too clever by half and too full of herself. She said she would not be coming to our wedding. We cut short the weekend and returned to Sheffield on the Saturday. I had seen her

irrational and unpleasant outburst like this many times before and had learned just to ignore them. But what a mixed-up unpleasant mess the Williams family must have seemed to Granny.

We carried on planning our future. I had a flat and Granny had a house. We sold both and bought a house.

We were married on the 3rd September 1977 in a Protestant church in Sheffield. The ceremony was painted in cartoon by Peter Hayes and can be seen in our downstairs loo. The reception was an informal affair in Mike and Mary Hayes' garden. The food was prepared by Stephen's wife Dale's parents. It was a nice spread and a good do. Ma told me it was horrible and nobody there liked her or talked to her.

We set off for Antigua that afternoon. We had a room with a veranda open directly onto the beach. We had a nice time and some very good memories. My bestie is the memory of snorkelling and swimming among the fishes in the coral reef. We have never had another long beach holiday. In due course we set off for home and for work.

Claire was born on the 7th May 1978. We had expected a boy all through the pregnancy although there was no reason to expect either girl or boy. We had referred to the baby as Oscar up to that day. It was not a nice birth. Claire was tiny, even allowing for her gestational age! I was worried that something would go wrong even though I had no reason to be worried about her. I suppose I just didn't want anything to go wrong. I did not tell Granny about my worries because she had gone through so much and was exhausted. Also, I knew my worries were unfounded. I said a prayer to myself asking that everything should go well. I've never done that since about anything.

The feeling of elation trumped the worry. It was the most powerful feeling of happiness of my life, before or since. I loved Granny so much more than I had done before. She had been so brave and strong and now she was just exhausted. She had gone through all of this because of me. I left her to get some rest and I walked happily back to our house. On the way home, I passed an Irish friend called Brendan. I had not seen him coming. As he approached me he said, "It has all gone well, then." I replied, "Yes, how do you know?" "It's written on your face."

I was impatient to get back to Granny. I went to her room. She was happy to see me. We had previously decided that, if by chance, we had a girl we would call her Claire. I got into the hospital bed beside Granny, dressed of course. Soon a big black nurse came into the room to check Granny and the baby. "Get out of that bed" she barked. I obeyed. Then, "What are you going to call this baby?" "Claire, we replied." "You can't call a baby Claire! It has to be Claire Louise." We both agreed and there it is.

After a few days, Claire and Granny came home. We fussed over Claire. We fussed far too much. She was in bed with us and we were getting little sleep. Peter Todd came to visit. He told us to put her in the other room by herself and allow her to cry for a while. It was excellent advice to overwhelmed parents, but contrary to modern medical opinion.

Family life trumped my medical duties. It was lovely being newlyweds and having our little daughter. We settled into parenthood quickly under Peter's orders.

I expected to be appointed as senior registrar at the Children's Hospital but the panel chose my co-registrar, Sue Illett, instead, so I needed to find a suitable job. I applied for a job in Canada. I was interviewed by phone and was successful.

We three set off for the New World. Claire was 7 weeks old.

Chapter 14
Kingston, Ontario

We arrived in Kingston in June 1978. We had arranged to rent a flat in a complex owned by the hospital. Everything was just right. Canadian summer is like the best of English summer weather. The people were informal and friendly. Kingston is an old city by Canadian standards. It's a handsome middleclass sort of place on the eastern shore of Lake Ontario. The famous old historic Fort Henry is sited there, built there to defend British settlers from the newly independent America. The fort overlooks Lake Ontario, just as it drains into the St Lawrence River. The Thousand Islands can be seen from Fort Henry. There is an impressive road bridge across the St Lawrence to upper New York State.

I was the Chief Resident to the paediatric department on a one-year contract. It was a lovely department to work in. There were 8 consultants, or staff members as they were called. All were good at their job and were approachable. There were 8 or so residents and many medical students. We would all meet in the morning to plan the day. The residents would describe each of the patients and the staff member in charge of that patient would outline his or her views, and these decisions would be debated by all and sundry. The staff members always treated the juniors and students with respect. It was so different to the typical English consultant of those days. We then went to see each patient on the ward where the staff member would listen to the mother's concerns and outline the plans for the day.

I particularly remembered one incident on the ward round. The most senior consultant was a really nice bloke called Don Delahaye. He was talking to a mother with a toddler on her lap. The child got off her lap and was sick on the floor. Don said, "Just wait there." He got a bucket and mop and a cloth, and he knelt down and wiped the floor clean. He waived the ward cleaner away saying he could manage. Instant respect!

Granny and Claire were happy. Granny quickly made friends in other flats, with the families of my colleagues and with Mike and

Sandra. Mike is the brother of her friend, Sheila, who she brought along to my hastily arranged home warming party in Sheffield. There was a sand pit in the hospital were Granny and several other mothers used to meet and Claire had a little Chinese friend there called Amy Kim. I used to come home after work each day and bath Claire. I used to get in the bath with her. One day I found myself sitting in the bath on one of her poos.

We were good friends with a pair of junior residents called Anna Timmell and Sandra Nehring. Sandra had been to finishing school in Austria and had had Sylvestor Stylone as a boyfriend. We liked Anna's name. We signed on the list of family doctors with one of my favourite staff paediatricians called Jan McConville. We became friends with Jan and her family.

We drove round Lake Ontario when Audrey and Alan came to visit. We stayed at a motel at Niagara Falls. We visited Ottawa and Quebec City and picnicked on the Plains of Abraham with our little toddler. Peter Hayes came over to stay and we spent a week in North Ontario near Perth where I acted as doctor to 50 children with cystic fibrosis. The camp was organised by the Ontario Society for Crippled Children, a title that would have been considered inappropriate by the politically correct English.

Winter was particularly interesting. It comes on suddenly. There is only a week or two between summer and winter. There are frequent snow storms. I would cycle to work through the snow. Sometimes I even skied to work. Going in at night, the temperature occasionally dropped to minus 40 deg C. which is also almost exactly minus 40 deg F. If it was minus 12 or above, Granny would wheel Claire up to the shopping mall. The snot and dribble on Claire's face would freeze. She would then pick it off her face and suck it as a lolly.

I started to apply for paediatric consultant posts in the UK. Granny wanted to stay near Sheffield so that she could continue in her post at the University. I did not want to work in the Sheffield Children's Hospital and nor did I think they would want me. I applied for a post in Chesterfield but was unsuccessful. We did not want to return to the UK with me unemployed. Granny agreed that we stay on in Canada for another year. Peter's dad, Jack Todd, contacted Granny to say that a post was being advertised in Worksop. He had given a lecture there and thought it would be a particularly nice place to work. I applied, and I accepted their invitation to be interviewed, only on condition that I would be paid full travel expenses including air fares, and that they deferred the appointment for one year. I wrote this because Chesterfield had said they would cover travel costs but then refused to reimburse air fares. That left us left severely short of money. I mentioned this dilemma about my finances one day at work. Don Delahaye heard about it and told me he would be pleased to lend me money; what a good chap.

I joined the team in the premature baby care unit as senior resident. I think it was probably the best baby intensive care unit in the world at that time. It had two outstandingly brilliant young staff members called Barry Smith and Keith Tanswell. It was led by a wise head of neonatology who was himself excellent and who did everything to facilitate Keith's and Barry's work; his name was

Wesley Boston. It was a great team and far, far ahead of English neonatal units.

We moved into a nice old house with a garden in our second year in Kingston. Claire was a little more than 1 year old. Granny was appointed as Professor at Queen's University and restarted teaching Law. I was welcomed into the neonatal team and loved the discussions with my senior colleagues there. And they seemed to like my ideas and contributions. I became very proficient with techniques for the care of the very sick new-born prems.

I was approached with an offer of a staff-grade post. That would mean I was on the equivalent to a consultant in the U.K, except that junior staff graders did not have guaranteed tenure of post. I was told my first year would be in their Moose Factory Hospital which was sited on the shores of Hudson Bay. The daily mean temperature is below 0 deg C for 7 months each year. I declined the offer which had little appeal to Granny or myself or even to Claire.

I would like to tell you one story which demonstrates how nice the seniors were. A pregnant black American lady was on holiday in Kingston and she went into premature labour at 27 weeks gestation. We delivered her babies who developed severe premature breathing complications. They needed high level care intensive care for months. A few days before they were ready to be discharged, I was walking round the ward checking the babies with Barry. He told the lady they could go home as soon as she was ready with her travel arrangements and that they would need to be followed-up by her paediatrician in the US. We moved on to the next patients. As we were about to leave, Barry said to me that he was going back to see the lady because she was crying and the nurses were consoling her. "What's your worry?", he asked. The head nurse passed a letter. It was a bill from the hospital for $10,000 or something like that. She explained that the family would be destitute for the rest of their lives. Barry said, "I'll deal with it." He tore the bill up in front of her and put it in the clinical waste. "Just drive off home." Nothing more was ever said about the matter.

Granny was pregnant again. She had a delightful obstetrician called Sonny. The pregnancy went well. Sonny conducted the delivery with considerable expertise. Out popped Anna, cried for a minute or two and promptly went off to sleep. Anna's name was chosen because we had known Anna Timmell and got to like her name.

Anna was born in the middle of the night. I walked down to the hospital in the morning with Claire to see mummy and Anna. Claire was singing as we walked, repeating over and over again "Babb'n Anna, Babb'n Anna, Babb'n Anna,....." I loved Anna every bit as much as I loved Claire at her birth, but nothing can ever match the ecstasy of a first delivery for a father, or so I think.

The house was perfect and quite near the hospital. The job could not have been better.

We did not see much of Babb'n Anna in Canada. She slept in her own bedroom, woke regularly for milk, smiled at all and sundry, burped and went back to sleep. We three were looking forward to meeting the real Anna! But nothing much has changed since!

The staff paediatricians held an end of year party for the residents. The leavers were called forward one by one to be thanked by Wesley Boston, the very wise head of department. I was last to be called. I walked forward checking that my flies were secure. I glanced Jan McConville's face as I walked. She was smiling at me and gently shaking her head as if to say, "You naughty boy." Wesley spoke quietly to me so that the audience could not hear. He told me that he had had considerable reservations about allowing me to stay on in the neonatal unit because he felt I was arrogant and opinionated. He said he quickly changed his mind when we started to work together, and he had come to think that I would become one of the very best consultant appointments of the year in the UK. What can one say?

Chapter 15
We're from Worksop, mighty, mighty Worksop!

We had a few days after arriving back in the UK before I had to start work in Worksop. We stayed with Vincent, then Alan and Audrey and Joe and Ma and, no doubt, other relatives. Anna was introduced to the family. Anna was a chubby, happy baby who smiled at almost anybody and anything. She was a delight. Claire was a strong character. I don't remember much about those visits but I do remember having dinner with Granny and Grandad Todd. Granny T was sitting at the end of the table, nearest to the kitchen. Claire was on her left, aged 2 and a quarter. Chicken was on the menu. Claire was struggling to cut her chicken. Granny T asked, "Can I help you?" "No." replied Claire as she continued her ordeal. Again, Granny T asked, "Oh do let me help." I beckoned to Granny T to desist but she took no notice. Again, she asked. Claire went into melt down. Granny carried a screaming Claire out of the room. I don't know if Claire ever got the chicken and that knife! Claire was generally a friendly, happy, obedient child but she did like to set her limits. Anna just smiled all through this.

I entered the paediatric ward in Worksop at 9.00 am prompt. I introduced myself to the sister i/c, Elaine Hollings. I told her that we were living in a house which the hospital had provided about 5 minutes walk from the ward. I was well aware I was being closely watched. There were several children in humidified oxygen tents. I could see that things needed to change.

I went on to the baby unit. (PS, I have just corrected one of my best of many spelling mistakes, younit!). The sister was a rather pious looking woman of late middle age and she did not strike me as one who would tolerate me meddling in her affairs. She knew how to run her unit and she didn't need any help. I was told to gown up and wear a mask. I did as told. The few babies looked fine but none were on drips or even had a feeding tube in their nose. Most were under phototherapy. I was shown all the babies and said little. Some were being fed with a contraption that I had never seen being used in the UK. It was essentially a glass feeding bottle with a teat at both ends. The milk flowed slowly into the mouth by gravity and could be accelerated if necessary by squeezing the upper teat.

It really was time to plan a future for Worksop paediatrics. I knew that my predecessor had been half-time in Worksop and the same in Doncaster. All the juniors were GP trainees with no preceding experience of paediatric care. Maternity care and care of the new-born persistently figured among the worst of any districts in the UK. Things needed to change.

I left the SCBU and went to see the babies on the maternity ward. I was stopped at the door by the sister in charge. "There's no need for you to come here unless you are invited. Mr VP runs the unit and the babies are under his care. Your juniors assist him. I will phone him and let him know that you are here. Wait here." Wow, I had not expected that! She returned in a few minutes. VP had given his permission for me to enter and she told me he would give me a call in due course. I knew there was a junior consultant obstetrician and was keen to meet him.

It was lunch time by now and I needed to think. VP waltzed into my office without knocking. He offered his hand and said, "V's the name." "Leonard.", I replied. "Well, I'm the boss in my department and you're the boss in yours; the babies in my unit are under my care and I have the right to call you any time I want. OK." " Yes, OK, if you really want it that way, but I want you to put that in writing, and, of course, I shall be scrupulously honest to any mothers whose child is admitted to the SCBU or paediatric unit with concerns about earlier care on your unit. I would like you to know that." He didn't linger long. I received his letter a day or so later. He had reconsidered anddecided it would be better if I were to be in charge of the babies.

There were further battles to be fought and I was prepared. Sister Hollings in the children's ward was a delight and entirely on my side. She wanted things to improve in her ward. We didn't always agree about the details but we agreed on the principle. Not all her nurses agreed and several resigned shortly after my arrival. I was welcomed into the maternity unit and started doing a ward round there once each week with all the juniors to teach them how to examine babies. Most of the midwives were pleased with the new arrangement.

It was not like that in the baby unit. Sister would not agree to any change. I phoned for one of the babies to be tube fed one evening. “No. Doctors should do that if they feel the need.” I came back to the ward and passed the tube myself. I gave the baby milk through the tube with two nurses watching and sister and another nurse talking to each other in sister’s office. The two nurses smiled at me as I left. One of them was a really beautiful middle-aged state enrolled nurse and the other was of higher grade, a state registered nurse. I sensed that there was division among the troops and that I had allies.

Things came to a head before too long. An unmarried mother turned up in well established labour at 27 weeks gestation. When her son was born he weighed about 900 grams and had respiratory problems. He could not feed without assistance and he needed help breathing. There was an old-fashioned ventilator on the ward which had never been used. I put him onto the ventilator and he improved. One of the nurses passed a feeding tube under my supervision. Another nurse knelt and prayed while we were doing this. She insisted that the baby be baptised. The chaplain invited mother in to pray together for him. The mother never set eyes on her child again. I don’t know what she had been told but my few early words to her were entirely encouraging.

I visited the baby unit early the next day. Sister was in her office and told me that she had asked another nurse to accompany me on the ward round. The baby was doing well and several of the nurses were taking an interest in him. Things were changing but I had not yet won.

I invited Professor Sir David Hull to visit the ward. He was professor of neonatal care in Nottingham and a well respected figure in British paediatrics. He had been on the panel that interviewed and appointed me. I told him about my troubles and about many of the rules such as wearing gowns and masks. I told him I was going to ask him in front of all the staff about procedures such as gowning up and feeding tubes. I invited sister to welcome him in and call me when he arrived. She seemed pleased. She was not pleased by the time he left. He supported everything I wanted and complimented her on orchestrating this difficult change for the unit. Shortly thereafter, she went off sick and then took early retirement.

Quite a few other nurses left but new ones took their posts and my battles in my department were won. The junior doctors enjoyed my input and my teaching and invited me to a dinner to thank me for the change. I met one of them again not too long ago at Lucy and Aurelio's wedding. We were seated together for dinner. He told me that he had been disappointed at being allocated to Worksop in his GP training programme but that that all changed when I arrived.

But there were further problems to be fought in the maternity department. I met someone who knew VP. He told me V was awful. He told me that V ordered every baby to be given only sugar water for the first 24 hours to stop hypoglycaemic attacks. He told me that every mother must have a chest Xray in early pregnancy to pick up undiagnosed TB, that every mother had to have a pubic shave and a rectal enema at the onset of labour to "keep things clean," that every first pregnancy had to have an episiotomy, and that every mother was allocated to a length of stay on the postnatal ward at the booking clinic of either 2 or 5 or 10 days depending on her perceived needs. There were still fights to be won but things were going my way.

Anna awoke to the world and was a joy to Claire and to Granny and myself. She was always happy. She loved playing with Claire and being told stories. She was very forward with talking but lacked confidence in her ability to walk. She could walk holding a length of wool if someone was holding the other end but she fell down on her bottom immediately if the other end was dropped.

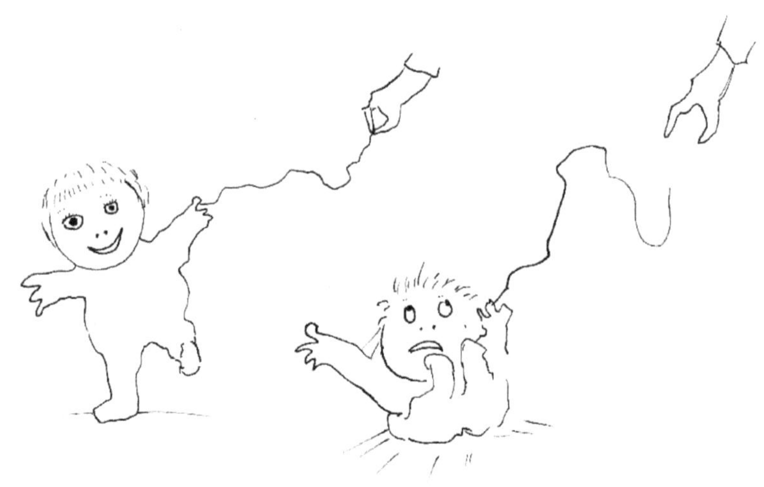

Sarah was born 2 years after Anna. She took command of the family right from the start. She did not want to sleep. She knew what she wanted and what she did not want and she formed plans for getting her own way. She would dismiss any of us if we tried to thwart her with shake of her head and the utterance of "Well anyway." If she liked something she said "dondee dondee." Granny and I would sometimes listen to the three of them planning to ask for treats, such as an ice cream. They told Sarah that she was the most likely to succeed and therefore she should make the request. In would walk a very cute little Sarah looking shy and submissive. She whispered her request as if she were too shy to ask.

Two years later, Rachel arrived. Granny broke all the maternity rules. She arrived in the labour ward about 10 minutes before Rachel's arrival. She declined a shave or an enema and she discharged herself about 6 hours after delivery despite being told by the consultant that she would likely bleed to death. Baby Rachel was a pest. She would not feed. She sobbed pathetically if anyone other than direct family came into the house. She was very happy playing with her sisters. This changed during the reception following grandad Todd's funeral. She started by pulling funny faces at her sisters to make them cheer up. Then she started doing the same to the other guests. She would crouch with her arms in front imitating the Incredible Hulk but with her figure she looked more like a daddy long legs standing up on its back feet. A few years later, she changed into a boy. She was called Roger because she found the name funny. That evolved into Roj, and then Poj, both said with a French accent.

I am not going to describe the lovely time that Granny and I had with our gorgeous girls. It was hard work but it was the most wonderful time of my life. They were great fun. It ended when Claire set off for University. We all drove home in tears.

The work in the hospital went incredibly well. The young trainee doctors loved being sent to Worksop. Our yearly statistics demonstrated we were doing very well compared to other districts in Trent Region. The Sheffield medical students attached to Worksop nearly all sang our praises. An article was written about me in the Sheffield Children's Hospital junior doctors magazine saying I was the consultant that they would most like to emulate.
I am going to finish this chapter with an account of the quite extraordinary sequence of troubles I got into at the hospital. But before that I want to tell you about one very proud event.

RDS is the dreaded, often fatal, respiratory disease of premature babies, properly called Respiratory Distress Syndrome. I attended a lecture about RDS in Nottingham. Various speakers presented their contributions. The main speaker spoke last of all and for much longer. He was Professor Neil Marlow, head of neonatology at UCH, and the top neonatologist in the country. He had made his greatest contribution by introducing a highly successful technique called High Frequency Oscillation Ventilation (don't fuss that you don't know what that means). He spoke of the history of the fight against RDS. I was thoroughly enjoying listening to stories about these famous paediatricians of the past, all of whom I had read about, and about how progress was made by "Standing on the Shoulders of Giants." He finished by moving on to his own contribution. He said he did not know the name of his giant, note the use of small g here, but he remembered his lecture. He said it was about a technique called Optimal CPAP. I knew he was going to talk about my friends, Barry and Keith at Kingston, who had developed Optimal CPAP and I felt a gush of pride for my erstwhile colleagues and friends. I sat back to listen and enjoy, and perhaps even to stand up and speak a little about them at the end. But it was not about Kingston at all. He described a lecture given in Sheffield in 1986 when he was a junior. He could not remember the name of the speaker but he said it had the most profound influence on him and essentially lead to the development of his understanding of RDS and to the development of his technique. GOSH!!! I had given that lecture. I did not dare stand up at the questions and comments session where the good and the great were applauding him for his contribution. A week later, I wrote to him, enclosing a copy of my lecture notes. You will find his gracious reply tucked into my Gray's Anatomy in the boys' room.

It makes me angry when I remember that the hospital banned me from using this technique a few years later because it was "unconventional and untested."

But now to the interesting bits. The first was a decision by the hospital administration to convert the house next door to us into a residential psychiatric unit. We lived in 36 Highland Grove. We were very close to number 34; a matter of about 2 meters. We had moved to our house because I was initially a single consultant, on call every day and night, with only three trainee GPs none of whom had any experience in paediatrics and we were regularly putting very low birth weight babies into our own intensive care. Our most dramatic survivor was a 23 week girl who required prolonged ventilatory support and intravenous feeding. The last I heard of her, she was at university and doing well but she was short. She was one of the most premature babies to have survived at that time; and I mean world-wide. The hospital administration knew all this and used to boast about our unit. However, going back to the house, they told us that they could not ensure our safety if we decided to stay at no. 36; both from fire risk and personal risk to the children from the inmates. They wanted to reduce costs by converting the two houses into one big unit. They told me they would like us to move to 4 Highland Grove; the two houses were valued at the same price. We solicited independent advice which advised us to accept the inevitable. The owners of number 4 had a plot of land directly adjacent to the house. It was really just their side garden. The hospital decided that this should not be part of the deal because it had value as a potential building plot. We were not happy.

The Chief Executive wrote to me to offer this plot to us for a modest rent "in perpetuity". I agreed and the plot became our vegetable garden. We were content.

A few years later a new Chief Executive, Munro, was appointed, Munro decided to cash in on the plot. He terminated my tenancy. I protested, but to no avail. I said I would move out of Highland Grove to a house about 20 miles away. He knew my contract stipulated that I must live within 22 miles of the hospital and he knew that the paediatric department would not function well if I were to do this. My newly appointed colleague would not have coped. I protested angrily.

There was nothing I could do. I did not want to jeopardise the department or to move a long way away just to spite him. I conceded shortly after.

Another, extraordinary allegation was made against me. I was asked to see a 2 or 3 month old baby by the social services because of bruises on the face. It looked to me like three finger marks on one side and a thumb mark on the other. When I placed my fingers and thumb on the marks the baby's nose and mouth were covered. I wrote a report describing the marks and wrote that I thought it likely that there had been an aborted attempt to smother the baby. It could not have been in play; considerable pressure would be needed to make such marks. A case conference was called and the police were involved. All the information distributed to attendees. I was invited to speak first, "Everything I know is in the letter and my conclusions are clear." The police were invited to respond. The officer did not agree with my conclusions. He had interviewed the parents and father had told him that the child had been sitting on his knee and had rocked forward; the father reached forward and grabbed the baby by the face in order to protect him. The father had acted the scene with a doll, and the officer acted it out to us. I said I did not believe this. Discussions followed. The chairman concluded the meeting, saying that he preferred the officer's report but that the child should be put on the at-risk register. I protested again. I did not agree with the police officer's view. I had vastly more experience of this type of work than he had. I pointed out that there was no other information to support poor parenting other than mine so if they decided to reject my opinion, there were no grounds at all to put the child's name on the at-risk register. They should not register the child as at-risk and yet say that they did not believe my explanation. I went home angry.

The baby died a few days after this. There were multiple bruises. The pathologist said the child had been smothered. Father was arrested. Father admitted smothering the baby. He said he was not the baby's father. The mother allowed him to pretend that they were a married couple and she really only tolerated him because he brought money into the house and he did all the household duties.

A serious case review was commissioned by Nottinghamshire Social Services and concluded that my inadequacy had caused the death of the baby. The chairperson said that the other members at the case conference had all thought I was joking, and that I was always too interested in child deaths.

I was called to a disciplinary panel by the Director of Social Services. I repeated what I had already said. I told them to re-read my contemporaneous report of the injury and re-read exactly what was minuted at case conference. Both clearly reported what I had said and in neither was there any suggestion that I had not been serious and clear throughout. The panel dismissed my arguments. They told me that their report would be widely distributed to all relevant professionals throughout the country.

Granny suggested that I contact her sister Mary. Mary wrote to the Director of Social Services saying that he should read the case conference report and my report very carefully once again. He would find no suggestion that I had been joking; on the contrary, the concerns I had expressed about parenting had been perfectly serious. That being so he should decide not to publicise his erroneous findings. If he were not to do so, we would pursue him for defamation. He conceded.

I was phoned by the paediatrician on the panel. He told me that he and other members of the panel had been persuaded by all the other members of the case conference team. He said my letter was clear. There was nothing in the minutes to suggest I had been joking and that I had challenged police officer's evidence. I never heard any more about the matter.

My next great scandal was even more outrageous. I was asked to attend a meeting of the 3 paediatricians, Jane, Henry and myself and a team from social services. The meeting was to be chaired by my colleague, Justin, a psychologist, and we were told that it was about improving the child protection service. There was to be an independent assessor. The three of us agreed to take part.

We arrived and made ourselves comfortable at a long table, with their team of about 6 on one side, the assessor at one end of the table and we three facing Justin and team.

Justin opened the meeting by saying that the social worker found the paediatricians difficult to work with. The social services would phone the paediatric secretary to ask for a child to be examined in order to decide if the parents had injured the child. The secretary would agree and suggest a time that was convenient, always on the same day. This convenience depended on what duties the on-call paediatrician had that day. For instance, the secretary would say well he/she will be in outpatients from 2pm to 5 pm and would therefore see the child shortly after 5. Justin said that was unfair to the family and to the social workers, because they worked long hours from 9 to 5 and did not like being kept waiting after their long days. The paediatricians should always see the children straight away as an emergency.

I responded that we had discussed this problem many times in the past and that there was no easy solution. We also had tight schedules and we also worked long hours. I pointed out that social services had agreed that all child abuse cases should be seen by a consultant and not by the juniors. We had agreed that we would come in early in the morning if asked, and would happily see cases at lunch time and as soon as work finished in the afternoon and at any time we were free. After some discussion the social worker who came to the meeting backed us up and we heard no more about it.

The next example followed a meeting in Nottingham arranged to celebrate the excellence of the child sex abuse services in the county and in S. Yorkshire. It had been arranged by the Department of Health in London. Various speakers from all over the area told the audience about the wonderful service we were all providing.

I stood up and explained that I had long been worried about the services we offered. I explained that I had been having meetings about the services with the senior police officers and paediatricians from surrounding districts including S Yorks. Essentially, we were each seeing one, two or three teenaged girls each year. Our main problem was that we never had the opportunity to examine normal girls of that age so it was hard to distinguish normal from abnormal. I said that if I ever had to present my views in court and my experience was interrogated the court would rightly dismiss my opinion because of lack of experience in the field. I explained all this to the delegates. There was a stony silence.

A week or so later I got a request from the medical director at Doncaster to meet him. He showed me the letter from the Department of Health to the Chief Executive which said my action was disgraceful and discourteous to the teams who worked so hard. It suggested I should be dismissed. I told him what I knew about the services both at Doncaster and Bassetlaw and that I had discussed the services with the paediatricians from the surrounding districts. The views I expressed were theirs as well as mine. He was totally satisfied. The Rotherham sex abuse scandal hit the headlines shortly thereafter. The Department of Health never mentioned it again.

I will say no more about Bassetlaw. You've had enough.

Chapter 16
Retirement

Granny was offered a generous redundancy settlement by the University which she accepted and she retired on the 31st October 2009, aged 59 yrs 2 months.

I had planned to retire when I was 65, but Granny's early retirement prompted me to tender my resignation straight away. I had to give 3 months notice which set my early retirement date around Christmas, only one month before my 65th birthday. I told my consultant colleagues and the nursing staff.

About 2 or 3 days later, I got a call from the hospital pensions office. The lady said that she advised me to come and discuss this with her. She asked me about my savings and my expenditure and she told me that she felt certain that the hospital would offer me part-time employment after my retirement. She explained that the default arrangement was that I would receive half of my pensionable allowance as a lump sum and the other half would pay a monthly pension for the rest of my life, but that I could opt to alter the proportion according to my needs. She pointed out that that Granny and I spent very little and we could continue to live very well on a reduced monthly pension. That would result in a bigger lump sum and if we had things we might like to spend a lot of money on in the short term, it might be better to opt for an enhanced lump sum. She pointed out that I would receive more total money with an enhanced lump sum if I were to die within seven years of retirement and more money in the end with enhanced monthly pension if I lived for more than 7 years. The other point she made was that I would not be able to change my option after I had tendered my resignation, and for that reason she had kept my resignation letter to herself.

Granny and myself discussed all this and decided to opt for a bigger lump sum, essentially because our daughters had finished university and were setting off on building their futures. I went back to my lady in the pensions department and told her our decision. She said that she had another suggestion. She had contacted the personnel department and that they had an offer of further employment for me. Essentially this was 2 days a week with no night duties working at Doncaster Hospital in outpatients and various other community medical matters for 1 year, on a renewable basis. I accepted that because I had not formulated any plans on what I would do in retirement. I thought retirement might be boring. I told the doctors and the ward that my retirement had been delayed for a month.

I had a good year working in outpatients in Doncaster. I worked with the Doncaster Education Board advising about appropriate education for children with a variety of conditions such as AIDS, severe cerebral palsy and terminal cancers. I was the medical consultant charged with investigating all the deaths of children in South Yorkshire and north Nottinghamshire. And I was the medical adviser to the children's Social Services. These were all very interesting jobs and I carried on doing it into the 2nd year.

In April 2012, I had a short episode of chest pain when I was carrying a suitcase. I had had trivial episodes before, hardly noticeable. I was aware that they may have been from my heart and went to see the GP. I was expecting to be sent away but he referred me for an exercise ECG. I went through the treadmill procedure with no pain at all and expected to be told it was nothing at all. But the nurse specialist told me that it was not normal and that she needed to arrange a cardiac catherization to visualise my coronary arteries. This was done and demonstrated a narrowing of the anterior coronary artery and I was referred to Sheffield for a stent. I was also told that I had moderate blood pressure and moderately high cholesterol levels. I was started on statins, antihypertensive drugs and an aspirin like drug to stop the formation of blood clots. I have taken them every day since without any ill effects. A stent was placed in my coronary artery in June 2012 with a minor complication. The stent occluded a small branch of my coronary artery and caused a small myocardial infarct (that is, death of a small portion of heart muscle, what is commonly known as a heart attack). That was quite painful for a few hours but has never troubled me since. I was sent home. I bought a bike and started an exercise programme.

I was off work for a week and, when I returned to work, I travelled to Doncaster by hospital taxi, rather than driving myself. A couple of weeks later, the hospital said that they were not willing to pay for the taxi. They would not relent so I resigned saying this was unfair. That made them reinstate the taxi service and I agreed to continue working. Two weeks later I felt that I ought to re-start to drive because I felt well and thought I might be over-reacting. In the following week, I fell off to sleep while driving, crossed the road and bashed into the curb. I am sure it was due to the sedative effect of the beta blockers. It was my first ever motoring accident. I have not had any accidents since then.

I continued in post till the end of that year and have not been employed since. I have cancelled my GMC registration and so I am no longer allowed to be employed as a doctor.

Retirement proper started on New Years day 2013. It was just like a holiday period at first. But then, as time rolled on, I realised that I had no importance any more. Nobody wanted my opinion any more. My life was for me and for Granny, but was devoid of any responsibility. I liked it when I was asked to do favours for others or to give medical opinions. I was content but somewhat bored. Granny wanted me to start doing something to pass the time, anything would do. I considered U3A, a bird watching group and Jane Bodden recommended a natural history group. Nothing appealed. Nothing with groups appealed. I realised that I don't like chatting and mixing in groups. But equally, I don't like talking to individuals except for short 5 to 10 minute chats about specific matters. I am quite happy meeting up with someone else or a couple for a natter as long as Granny is with me and as long as it does not happen too often. I like people in general and almost never dislike anyone. I wish them well and will have short good-hearted chats but only for very short periods. I think people find me usually rather off-putting and trivial, sometimes interesting and different but always unpredictable. But the only relevant question for me was, "what could I do for the rest of my life that I would feel was at least partly interesting and challenging."

I decided to rent an allotment from the council. I set myself a challenge to produce sufficient amount and range of vegetables to feed Granny and myself all the year round and to do it using only tools that would have been available to me as a teenager.

I looked at the council website and found that there were plenty of sites available. I chose one at random. I phoned the steward and got a plot. The plot was overgrown and needed digging all over. This took me a week. The other people seemed friendly but uninspiring. I planted various things including an asparagus bed and globe artichokes. The Steward told me that those vegetables would not grow. I heard him but took no notice of much that he said. He did make quite an effort to help me and in many ways he was helpful but he tended to insist that I ought to accept his advice. My view was that I would listen to him but decide for myself. I planted pak-choi, which he didn't think would grow, but they did.

I like going down there and have a few good sensible mates. I usually cycle there and back when I don't have too much to carry. It has been very successful. I produce enough green veg to feed us all through the year. We get a fair amount of salad and a good supply of fresh fruit and nuts from the end of June to early December.

I was the first to grow asparagus and artichokes on the allotment and now several others are following suit. Recently, I have been propagating fruit trees by grafting and nut trees by layering. Hopefully, this year, my 7 year old mulberry tree will fruit. That will arouse interest but there will not be enough fruit to share with others for a few years.

I do all the gardening at home and the garden looks better than ever this year. I am gradually moving from plants to shrubs which require much less attention.

I do a few wood-work projects and some repair works around the house.

I seem to have found the right balance between work and doing nothing. I hope it will continue for a long time. The best thing of all is that I enjoy being with Granny. She feeds me well and we have many interesting conversations and debates. We squabble a bit but never really fall out with each other. We always chat together in bed in the morning while drinking our tea and coffee. She seems content with me and her life.

We used to go off on week-end breaks together but that has died down over the last three or 4 years. Granny is too busy with her various U3A roles. I used to enjoy our short breaks together. We have been on interesting holidays with the Keenans and with our friends John and Jenny, but I preferred the short breaks with Granny.

As I write this, we are in our 5th week of lock down because of the Coronavirus. I'm very interested in the science of the epidemic. There have been very few cases in Worksop and the population has been behaving very well. I expect it will reach us in time if there is no progress on an effective vaccine and that Granny and more so myself will be at high risk but it does not worry me. It may do if I catch the virus; I would not like to be admitted to an ITU. I wrote to Newsnight and our MP saying that the level of ordinary medical care in Care Homes is inadequate because coronavirus gives a pneumonia and the basis of treatment is the continuous administration of oxygen at the right level which can only be assessed with an oxygen saturation monitor, a cheap and easy to use bit of equipment. Neither the MP or Newsnight acknowledged my comment. I also pointed out that the government repeatedly quoted the R number as 0.5 to 0.9 but by my calculations it was around 0.94. Newsnight led with their own assessment of the R number the next night and their figure was close to mine. But they did not acknowledge me.

I think Granny finds the lock down harder than I do but she is coping and is pretty good humoured about it most of the time. I hope I don't die of coronavirus but I am not afraid of it. I think Granny feels the same. We would like to carry on a few more years and we are both moderately fit at present. I have come to terms with my status in society and I am content to be just part of the crowd.

The thing we miss most at this time is our 4 daughters and their families.

Chapter 17
Am I normal?

I am happy. I have always been happy. I have been very lucky in life. I have been given so much opportunity to do the things I want to do. I have seen and done such an array of things. But I am aware that I am odd. But I don't feel odd in myself; I feel normal. I have often been told that I am odd or weird by nice people who don't mean to be offensive, so I accept that there may be some truth to the statement.

I know I am a mixture of talents and weaknesses, just like everyone else. I know there are paradoxes. I am poor at spelling and reading and writing, yet I'm fairly fluent in speech. I did well in written examinations at university but I can't write an academic paper. I don't get jokes as well as others. I almost never ask someone to do me a favour or help me, but I like to be asked for help and to do favours. I don't want to dress well or look good because I don't want to draw favourable attention to myself. There are very few people who I really do like and almost none who I dislike. I don't have a single friend[4] and nor do I want one. The last time I had a friend was when I was at university. I meet him from time to time and I am still very comfortable with him. I find our family gives me more than enough friendship so I have no need to look outside. I am particularly fascinated by the grandchildren. I am enormously impressed by their huge range of diverse talents and I am proud of the way that their parents work to facilitate and encourage these developments.

People have suggested that I should go out and have a drink and a chat with them. I never agree because I don't want to be alone with them. If Granny and I were to be asked, I would go. I am fairly good at chatting with strangers and people I don't I don't know well but I rarely get any pleasure from doing so.
It is a funny thing that most normal people think of themselves as socially inadequate. Self-assessment of one's own personality

---

[4] Granny's comment: This is not quite true. Grandad had 2 people he called friends, both coincidentally called John. One lives in Worksop and one in London.

tends to be much more extreme than assessment done by others. Confident people tend to assess themselves as better than others and less confident persons do the opposite. I feel I have some lack of confidence in certain situations but I also feel I am very confident in other situations. I am probably more often over confident than under confident.

I remember feeling socially isolated at my very first school. It was so distressing that my mother took me out of that school and sent me to my grandmother's school. Later, when I was at the Catholic school, I felt very alone and very sad. I was removed from that school and settled well at Littlegrove School, an ordinary junior school. I was happy at boarding school and at university and fitted in well with most of my colleagues. I had friends in both schools and at university but I never kept in contact after I left. I remember one incident at university. I was chatting with one of my colleagues and he told me that he and a group of students had been discussing the psychology of the rest of us. I asked what the group made of me. He replied something like, "They could not get their heads around you. They didn't understand you. They just said you were weird." I wasn't upset at all; I was just interested. Similar comments have been made in some the jobs I have done and by many people. It does not worry me, just interests me.

The most unusual factor in my life was my early upbringing. Ma did all the upbringing. She was nice to us most of the time and I think she tried her best in very difficult circumstances. She felt that the English looked down on her and her only friends were Catholics who she met at church. Her in-laws offered friendship but she did not like them. She felt she had to behave in their boring "ever so nice" fashion. She had little money. She found life difficult and was admitted to a psychiatric hospital on one occasion in 1950. It was always referred to as a nervous breakdown. I don't know any more about it.

Joe was away at sea and, when he was on leave, he was less than helpful; in fact; he increased her stress levels. He liked to visit his mother and siblings. He would often go out to pubs. He didn't help in the home and almost never played with us children. He liked doing building jobs. He was thought charming and funny, particularly by the ladies. He liked flirting but I don't think it ever went further. He did like to take us to Hadley Wood where he would often hire a rowing boat. I think he did it, not so much for us, but because it was to do with boating.

Mary told me about an event that rather sums up his parenting skills. One day he took Mary with him to the pub in her push chair. The publican told Joe that minors were not allowed inside pubs. Joe protested but to no avail. Eventually, he asked if there was a room in which Mary could stay while he had a drink. The landlord showed him a small pantry. Joe popped Mary into the pantry in her push chair. She started crying so he closed the door and went into the pub for his drink. He wheeled her back home when he had finished. Joe liked to be the centre of attention and was happy to be made fun of. But as a parent, he was really rather redundant.

Mary was the closest to Ma but I think Vincent was her favourite. I was more independent. I kept on good terms with her by helping in the garden and with decorating the house but I also got into more trouble with her by doing exactly what I wanted to do. I think all three of us were happy. We bullied Mary too much, especially me.

Ma and Joe did not tell us stories or read to us. I never remember sitting on her knee other than when I had hurt myself. We had to go to church every Sunday and feast day and we had to take holy communion and go to confession every fortnight.

I felt a certain need to be cautious with Ma. I would prefer her not to be too aware of what I was up to. I did not confide in her. Essentially, I tried to do enough to keep her attention off me and I think that suited her because there is no doubt that she had a hard job as a single mother looking after three children. I don't think I ever had a meaningful conversation about anything at all with Joe. I could have a laugh with Joe and I could tease him, and that could be fun but nothing serious was ever discussed.

A particular influence on my personality might have been the repeated changes in teaching establishments and in the places in which I lived. I went to grandma's school in Finchley so I had no friends who lived nearby. I did have local friends when I went to Littlegrove for 3 years but I lost them when I went off to Worcester. I had friends at Worcester, most of whom lived near to Worcester and the boarders lived all over the country so we did not meet in the holidays. Ma and Joe moved to Hampshire and I had no friends there during the holidays. Similarly, I had friends in University during my six years training but we did not meet in the holidays. Then, for the next ten years, I moved to 11 different hospitals in the UK, Zambia and Canada before finally settling in Worksop. One gets used to making tenuous relationships and then moving on.

I was never told why I was sent to Worcester. It would have been much cheaper to let me go to Barnet Grammar. It may have been a genuine attempt to improve my prospects in life. If I had stayed at home, I doubt I would have ever worked hard enough to enter university. Both Joe and Ma had some interest in education, although neither would be described as educated. Also, Joe had been very impressed by the headmaster at Worcester, Mr Brown. G K Brown, or Godfrey as he was always known as, had won a gold and silver medal in the 440 yards relay and individuals race in the 1936 Olympic games in Berlin. I have a suspicion that the real reason I was sent to Worcester was that I was becoming more defiant and feral at home and that Ma had difficulty in coping with me. It may also have been that I might be a support to Vincent who had not settled in well at the school.

While I had not wanted to be sent off to Worcester, there is no doubt that it changed my life for the better. Without Worcester, I would not have become a doctor, would not have met Granny, none of you would have existed, and goodness knows what the outcome would have been. I very much doubt it would have matched all the wonderful things that have happened to me.
What is the legacy of my early upbringing?

One minor legacy is my poor literary skills. I used to occasionally read comics as a child because others did but I was never really interested in make-believe. I read gardening manuals and information about rearing cage birds and other animals. I read a few Enid Blyton books but without much interest. The first book I really enjoyed was The Old Man and the Sea by Ernest Hemingway; I think I was about 14 at the time. I think I would have had more interest if we had been read to as children. Poor literacy skills have been a minor handicap in my studies and work. One result of this was that I rarely had the confidence to write an academic article and nearly all the medical discoveries I made were written up by my juniors or others.

There is a funny story about that. A pair of twins were presented to me for examination by a social worker because each had a fractured arm and bruises. I diagnosed child abuse and was called to court to present my evidence. The defence team engaged Dr Colin Paterson whom I had never heard of. I was presented with 4 or 5 of his published articles to show that babies could spontaneously develop fractured bones and bruises without any trauma. He had named this condition "Temporary brittle bone disease." The papers backed up this claim. I was given them about 30 minutes before I had to give evidence and to be cross examined on them. I told my barrister that I was not prepared to comment before I had studied them and thought about them and that would take me a few days. The defence team argued that I should be up-to date with such important research and that there should be no delay. The judge was angry but eventually decided to adjourn the session for one week.

I found out that Dr Paterson was not a paediatrician, but that he spent a lot of time defending parents who had been accused of harming their children. He said the condition was called temporary brittle bone disease and that it was common but rarely recognised by paediatricians. He wrote up a series of 22 babies with temporary brittle bone disease. The condition affected infants for a few months in infancy during which any bones could just spontaneously break with no or minimal force. He wrote that paediatricians had argued that all these babies had been abused by a parent but that he had proved in court that these babies had his temporary brittle bone. He wrote that all these babies had done well after being returned to their families.

I phoned up several paediatricians and spoke to some that he had opposed. All told me that they thought the courts had taken the wrong decision. They told me he presented an eloquent plausible argument that convinced the judges. But they still believed that the children had been abused. I spoke to one of the paediatricians who worked in the same hospital as him. He told me that Paterson had lied in that paper. One of the 22 babies died shortly after the court case and the paediatricians and the police believed the child might have been murdered; what was absolutely clear was the child had not done well, but his paper reported that all the children had done well.

The defence barrister had sent the X-rays of the children to a paediatric radiologist in Liverpool for review. I asked to see her report but he said I could not because he was not going to present it in court. I phoned her and asked for a full copy of her report. I explained that I was in court and that Paterson was defending the family. She refused saying that the barrister had told her that on no account could she share her report about my twins with anyone and that because he had paid for the report, it belonged to him, and him alone. I protested but to no avail.

The court restarted the following week. I told my barrister and he said that the radiologist had no right to refuse; in fact, she had a duty to share information. We confronted the defence barrister just before the session opened and told him we were going to report all this to the judge. He hardly cross examined my evidence at all. He looked terrified. We won the case and the children were taken into care.

I decided to write this up because Paterson had lied in his paper and his interventions were putting children's lives and risk. I handed my article to the President of the College of Paediatricians. I heard nothing more for a few months. Then Granny came home one day and told me that my article had been passed on to her because it was very important but needed to be written out properly, and could she please redraft it. Apparently, the President had sent my article to his legal team who said it should be worded more cautiously by a lawyer. Granny was asked to write it out properly. (They obviously had not twigged that I might know Granny.) Granny redrafted the article and received great acclaim. No mention of me was made in her article.[5] She was invited to present her article as the Guest Lecturer at the most prestigious paediatric conference in the UK, the Cambridge Paediatric Conference, held in King's College. I would not have

[5] Granny's comment: Grandad's recounting of this is not entirely accurate. For a different version, see my autobiography!

been able to get a place at this conference but the guest speaker was allowed to take a friend, and I was chosen as her pretty bimbo. Paterson was subsequently struck off the medical register.

To my mind, the most obvious reason that people think me weird is that I won't engage with others as a friend. I think I am seen as friendly and likeable by many people and on a few occasions in my life I have found these people really interesting. But I still shy away from them if they appear to want to become friends. There have been a few people in my life that I would have liked to make, or to keep, as friends, but shied away from.

In a way, I did this with Granny. At our first meeting, when she invited me to dinner with her cousin Peter, I decided to ask her out but rather than doing that I chose to say I was arranging a house-warming party. Up to that evening, I had no intention of arranging such a party, but it seemed a convenient way of arranging another meeting. Fortunately, she pushed the agenda forward by phoning to ask when this party was to take place. I was pleased because it gave me another chance to meet her and it was a clear declaration of interest on her part. I had time to build up courage to ask her out and I had no internal excuse not to do so.

I like being asked to do things for others but find it difficult to ask others to do things for me. This goes back to my childhood. Ma would ask me to do thing and I liked doing them for her. She would be nice to me because I had done something for her. But I learned to be cautious about asking her to do or get anything for me. I did ask her on occasions and she often became cross, saying I was being too greedy. I then felt ashamed for having asked. I avoided this by asking for money for birthdays and Christmas and leaving the amount to her or just saying that I did not want anything.

One facet of my way of talking that can irritate others in conversations is that I look to the other side of any discussion; if you say it is white, I'll say it is black. Granny is much more rigid in her views; Trump is bad, no question. I don't believe that people are either good or bad. Nor that people are clever or stupid, nice or horrid, etc. Most of us are both. We are on spectrum and each individual varies along that spectrum both in position and in time.

So I find no difficulty in believing that Trump has been good today but will be bad tomorrow. My daughters will remember my medical textbooks annotated with comments such as, "I don't agree with this.", "No!, That must be wrong. Look at my comment on Page X". I argue with myself, silently in my head, about almost everything. I search for an absolutely correct interpretation and accept that absolutely correct can never be achieved. My opinion base builds all the time and it can go backwords or forwards. At the moment, for instance, I am struggling with my tendency to overwater plants which I do because I have a fear of underwatering. It is all about the best balance. I find it hard to believe that others do not think in the same way.

I do tell lies from time to time but never to gain advantage or to hurt someone; they are just for fun. For instance, do you believe that I really and truly did go to India when I was a student, or is it just a lie?

I don't like spending money on myself. Most of my clothes are second hand. I buy new shoes but cheap ones and I don't like looking "smart". I buy woodworking tools but usually cheap ones. I buy better quality gardening because they last longer.

I am pleased after ex-patients come up to me to say how good I had been to them but I find it uncomfortable and embarrassing at the time.

I often think of my death or that of Granny's. If she were to die first, I would miss her greatly and I would think about her and talk to her in my head. I would be very surprised if I remarried. I think I would live alone and would be quite happy by myself. I would not like to die before Granny because despite her protestations to the contrary,[6] I think she would miss me even more than I would miss her. But she would cope better. We talk openly about this from time to time and neither of us feels gloomy about our futures.

So, to answer the question, "Am I normal?", my answer is a provisional yes. I am not perfect and nor do I want to be, but I'm

---

[6] Granny's comment: I always said to Grandad that I would prefer to die first, as I would miss him more than he would miss me!

satisfactory, I'm good enough. I have had a great life and I have enjoyed it. I'm just a bit weird.

17/5/2020

Autobiography of Catherine Williams nee Todd

22 August 1950 – date

Introduction

With apologies and love to my siblings Alison and Stephen, for revealing some of their childhood secrets!

This is dedicated to all my wonderful grandchildren. I can safely say they are the best in the world.

Dear Grandchildren,
Max came up with the idea that I should write a history about my life whilst Covid19 stops lots of things happening. I thought this was an excellent idea, so here is my life story. What follows is what I remember, or for when I was little, I have been told about myself. But before that starts I am including a history written by my eldest sister, Janet. This gives some background information on both my parents, your great-grandparents, and also some of one of your great-grandfather's earlier family.

Janet's Family History

I* (this, of course, is Janet writing) am writing this as an addition to the information that is already available, such as my Grandfather's memoir (*grandchildren, I, Catherine, have a copy of this*) and the family tree (my brother Stephen has done one). I will try and bring things up to date without going over old history which can be found elsewhere. Grandad writes of himself and the Todd family so I will put in what I remember of the Winters.

The Winters were merchants in Halifax around 1800. Later they had a firm manufacturing whale oil called Spermoline. This was sold later and became part of Shell. My Granny, Winifred Winter, was the eldest daughter. There were three more girls (Elsie, Jessie and Edie) two boys (Norman and Douglas) and then Rhoda. Norman and Douglas went into the family business but quarrelled. I never met Douglas but Aunt Edie had sided with Norman and I met him and his wife, Katy, several times at Bridge House. Katy had been a chorus girl and even when I knew her, and she must have been in her seventies, she wore lots of make-up and had bright yellow hair. This was unusual in the middle classes in the early 1950s. I gathered that she had been much disapproved of and I think this was part of the quarrel. I liked them both. They were kind and slightly raffish. Norman used to give me alcohol to drink and tell me unsuitable jokes.

The next sister, Elsie, married Ted Athey, who was also in the oil business, and they had one girl, Peggy. Elsie died when Peggy was about seven and she was looked after by Aunt Edie and my grandparents between them. My grandparents wanted to adopt her, but this was refused. When Peggy was ten Ted Athey remarried. Peggy remained with Aunt Edie, though she used to go and stay with her father and her stepmother and half sister.

Some time around 1890 my great-grandfather, James Winter, bought Bridge House in Little Haven, Pembrokeshire. This was a substantial four bedroomed house and it was used as a holiday cottage by the Winter family. When he died Edie inherited the house, which she lived in with Peggy and Jessie, who enjoyed ill health. Jessie married quite late to Jimmy Bowen-Rowlands who was Recorder of Liverpool. I do not think they ever lived together, but he used to visit Little Haven. Jessie lived into the 1950s and I remember her and how Aunt Edie used to fuss over her. Rhoda married Gwyn Evans and they lived on the Gower when I knew them, Uncle Gwyn was very Welsh and always had a cigarette dangling from the side of his mouth.

Dad

Dad's name was Allan Winter Todd. Allan for his father's brother who died in 1901 in South Africa and Winter as his mother's maiden name. He was born on 3 March 1903 and was the eldest of five children. Next was Douglas, about three years younger, then Oliver David, another about three years and then the twins, Jack and Joan, who were ten years younger than him.

Oliver died at the age of 10 months from measles. Grandad told me this once but he was never otherwise mentioned. Douglas died at the age of 20 very suddenly from pneumonia and remained an often mentioned sorrow to Grandad.

Dad never said much about his childhood. I have had the feeling, from a young age, that he was the least loved of the children, and my sister Alison thinks the same. Certainly I remember Grandad telling stories of Douglas and the twins but I remember none about Dad. I know he went to Manchester Grammar as did his brothers (and Joan's husband, David Valentine, who was in Jack's class and a great friend of his). Dad also belonged to the Boy Scouts as did his father and brothers. The Scouts were founded in 1908 and Grandad joined very early on, and Dad as soon as he could. He belonged to the First Davenport troupe where he met his lifelong friend, Arthur Coxson, who later became my godfather. He was awarded a prize by Baden-Powell (founder of the Scout movement) of one of the teeth of some animal (was it a tiger?) which had been made into a necklace and was a great honour. I don't know what for and Dad had no idea what had happened to the tooth.

Dad enjoyed Manchester Grammar. He was clever but not good at games as his brothers were – nor interested in them. He won a scholarship in 1921 to Wadham college Oxford and read PPE. I have found a photo of him in a rowing crew at (presumably)

Oxford. He is fourth from the back and I assume was in the Wadham crew. He got an upper second BA (firsts were quite rare) and a fellowship to Wisconsin University to read Economics.

When Dad spoke about his youth it really started in America. He arrived in 1924 and seems to have loved it from the moment he landed. He always sparkled when he spoke of America. In the first few days he went to a self-service restaurant where he sat and waited to be served, having never seen such a place. The same thing happened in shops and he was always finding new things. For the rest of his life he thought America was the greatest country in the world, and New York the greatest city. There is an interview with Dad in the University newspaper for October 1924, shortly after he arrived in America. It is to be found in the family information box and is largely about how beautiful the Wisconsin girls are and how free and exciting the place is after Oxford and England.

He arrived during Prohibition and had stories about it. He seems to have enjoyed breaking the law and said everyone did it. He used to say you could not go to dinner with a Bishop without being offered bootleg hooch, and you had a special knock for various speakeasies and were inspected before being let in. He had a store of songs from this period and used to sing them with his eyes twinkling. His favourite was 'Sweet Hortense'. This gem went

Tother day
I met a jay
His name was Hez e ki ah
I had to grin
To hear him chin
About his hearts' de si ah
I said I bet
Your little pet
Is nothing but a pure vam pi ah
He said now hey there pal
She aint that kind of gal

Oh my sweet Hortense
She aint good looking but she got good sense
Before

I kiss Hortense
I always buy a nickels worth of pepperments
She's got dandy teeth in her mouth
One points North and the other points South
Oh she is immense
You never met a girl like sweet Hortense

At the University Dad belonged to a fraternity called Zeta Psi. This was a chapter of one founded at New York University in 1847 and he had the sign as a small tattoo on one of his arms.

Dad was awarded an MA in Economics from Wisconsin in June 1925 (it is odd that he is in the year book for 1926) and then started work as a financial journalist in New York. He enjoyed himself and had lots of girlfriends, many of whom he remained in touch with for years. One story from this time is of Dad crossing the Atlantic in Second (possibly Third?) Class and meeting a girl in First Class where he spent the rest of the voyage and where a rumour circulated that he was an English Lord. I think he must have been very attractive with his bright blue eyes and wavy auburn-brown hair. When I was at school the girls all thought him very good looking and he was often compared to John Mills, a film star of the time. My brother Stephen and son Philip both went to the USA when young and stayed with one or more of Dad's old girlfriends.

I had thought Dad spent several years in New York but it can only have been about eighteen months at most because his brother Douglas died in February 1927 and Dad went home to his parents. He would have stayed in America and was going to apply for American citizenship, but for the death, and I think he would have returned but for the Depression which started in 1929.

Dad continued as a financial journalist in London. I don't know whom he wrote for except that, when he married in January 1938, he was editor of 'Industrial Britain', the journal of the Travel and Industrial Development Association of Great Britain and Northern Ireland. He lived in Chelsea and his brother Jack joined him when he became a medical student in about 1930. He was a member of the Labour party and was a candidate for the local council in about 1934 and treasurer of the Chelsea Labour Party in the late 1930s.

During the 1930s Dad went on many holidays and there is a splendid account of one visit to Italy with 'J' (Jack?). He loved Paris and visited often. He spoke good (though rather slow) French and some Italian. In the Summer of 1935 he went with Arthur Coxson and other friends to Germany. There they met Nazis for the first time and, when he returned, he immediately joined the Territorial Army as he thought, even then, that there was going to have to be another war.

At some point in the 1930s my parents met. Mother's brother Rodney was also a medical student at St. Thomas'. He was a year behind Jack and they were never friends, but they were both in the Rugby team for St. Thomas' and I think in the United London Medical Schools team. I think Mother and Dad saw each other at Rugby matches and they both went to Hospital social events. Mother told me that she first really noticed Dad when he was dancing. He was doing it so badly and so clearly enjoying himself that she thought 'What a nice man'. They married on 15 January 1938. That day there was a very high wind and, as they came out of the Church, Mother's veil blew into Dad's face. A photo of this made many newspaper front pages.

For their honeymoon they went to France to ski, which was a very unusual and adventurous thing to do at the time. I am sure this was Mother's choice, and she had been before. Dad told me he was very bad at skiing (as I would have expected). There seem to have been few or no ski lifts and Dad told me of toiling uphill with his skis and being passed by a very small child skiing effortlessly downwards.

My parents returned home to a rented flat in Cheyne Walk, Chelsea. Dad continued as a journalist and my brother Paul was born on October 14th 1938. Dad was very proud of himself over this because of the date in relation to their marriage.

War was declared in September 1939. Dad was already called up as he was by now a sergeant in the Territorial Army. He ended the war as a captain. He became a gunnery instructor and never left the UK, although he moved around quite a bit, mainly in Wales. At one time he was in Manorbier and was in charge of the defence of the beach, where sentries were posted. Dad organised a crab and lobster fishing enterprise by the sentries, who otherwise had very little to do. Mother followed him around with Paul and me and stayed in rented rooms. In the latter part of the war they were more settled and I think they spent about the last two years in Bettwsycoed.

After the war he went back to journalism, joining the Financial Times in about 1950. He started the column 'Finance and the Family'. At this time there were problem pages in women's magazines but I think this was the first one on finance. He was also the first person to get a child to review a play. Stephen and Catherine reviewed two Christmas shows in the late 1950s and made headlines. I remember one saying 'New recruits to the Butchers of Fleet Street'. Dad was given young people to train when they joined the Financial Times, among others Shirley Williams (later Labour MP and the Sec. for Education who started comprehensive schools), Nigel Lawson (later Chancellor of the

Exchequer) and William Rees-Mogg (father of Jacob) later Editor of The Times.

Dad was always interested in religion, or rather Christianity and Judaism, I don't remember any discussions on other religions. He read quite widely about this and was a member of the Unitarian Church who took his beliefs seriously. He was very much against the Catholic Church and used to make lots of jokes about the Pope. Mother was high C. of E. and much later converted to Catholicism. Both parents stuck to their own beliefs and argued about religion in their usual loud and disputatious way.

Concerning Dad's jokes, they were totally insensitive and he had no understanding of how other people felt. When my sister Alison (the third girl) was born he sent Mother a card with a black-bordered envelope (a sign of mourning). My cousin Sukey had a baby when at the end of University and refused to marry the father. This was in the mid 1960s, when illegitimacy was a real disgrace. After Beccy's birth she changed her mind. Dad, I and Alison went to the hastily arranged wedding, so that the baby could be registered as legitimate. At the reception, in front of both baby's parents, he said it was good to see the baby as 'we were all expecting it to be black'. This was at a time when colour prejudice was so rife it was unrecognised and it was common, and lawful, for landladies to advertise rooms with 'No Blacks'.

Having mourned the arrival of Alison, Dad very soon became enamoured of her. When he arrived home he used to call 'Where's Alison, she's precious and her Daddy loves her'. He never said these words about the rest of us and showed no sign of understanding that we might feel upset by this.

Despite his insensitivity, Dad got very emotional in films and I remember him crying throughout a showing of 'A tale of Two Cities'. He cried over books too – one of his favourites was 'Little Lord Fauntleroy' and another 'The Cloister and the Hearth'. He also cried with laughter – he was quite helpless during 'Airplane'.

Mother

My mother, Audrey Margaret Smith, was born on 11 March 1911. She was the daughter of Dr Edwin Smith and his wife, Edith nee

Dyer. There is a family tree of sorts, compiled by my Aunt Gill, in the information box with all the other family information. I know very little about the Dyers except for the fact that Edith's father Henry was a bigamist. The story is that Edith and her sister Nell were the first family and therefore legitimate. This was very important at the time. The story is also that Henry Dyer was a dubious business man who used to start up companies and then go bankrupt with large debts and then start another business. All I know about the Smiths is that Edwin came from Scotland.

Edith was a violinist and Edwin Smith was a general practitioner in Balham. The family lived in a large house on Balham High St. at the end of Balham Park Road. By the time I lived on the road the house had been demolished and replaced by a large block of flats. As was usual at that time, the doctor's surgery was part of the house. Edwin was also lecturer in forensic medicine at St. Thomas' Hospital and later became coroner for North East London. He qualified both as a doctor and a barrister. He was an early member of the Magic Circle, which was founded in 1906 by 23 amateur and professional magicians. He was a member of the inner magic circle which is still a great honour in the world of magicians.

Mother played the piano, passing Grade One at the age of four and playing in her first concert at five. There is a large book of newspaper cuttings about her with all the other information. She felt that she had been pushed into performing by her mother. She idolised her father and never blamed him for this, but reading the cuttings there is much more mention of him and lots of interviews with him. I have found no interview with her mother. Mother's childhood career was distinguished and she played at some important venues. She played at the Albert Hall with a full orchestra at the age of ten. One of the last concerts was at the London Palladium.

When she was eighteen, in 1929, Mother gave up playing in public. She had grown to detest this and wanted to stop practising all the time and do something else. She had always wanted to join the Guides, for instance and there had been no time for such things. She had loved maths but had not been able to study it properly. I am not sure what came next. I had thought she went to a college to study to be an auctioneer, estate agent and surveyor then but she did not qualify until 1937 so she must have done something else first. She told me she had a building firm and she told me about sending the apprentices out to buy striped paint and I think this must have been then.

Mother went to a college in Lincoln Inn Fields in 1934, when the college consisted of 400 men and her. She gained her degree in the Summer of 1937. This was an internal degree which was recognised by the University of London in 1938. The college was called the Auctioneer and Estate Agents Institute, later becoming the Royal Institute of Chartered Surveyors. This seems a much better name for it, since it was always largely about surveying, though Mother told me she had conducted some auctions.

Mother married Dad on 15 Jan 1938 and I have written what I know about their courtship in the section on Dad. She had a varied career which is summarised in the following paragraphs.

Paul was born in Oct. 1938. I followed in March 1940, by which time the Second World War was well underway. Mary, Alison, Stephen and Catherine followed, Catherine in August 1950. During this time Mother did no paid work – you could hardly say no work! – but when Catherine was five and starting school Mother developed polio. She was the local Guide Captain and was testing a child who was unwell. She was developing polio and Mother caught it off her. She had some paralysis and was in hospital, though she never needed a respirator. She decided to work for her ARCM, as this would qualify her to teach in a school, and quickly passed this. She started work as a music teacher at Bishop Simpson school in 1956. Not very long afterwards she was asked to take a maths class as the teacher was off sick. Mother found she enjoyed this much more than teaching music. Her surveyors' degree qualified her to teach maths and she switched to this.

Bishop Simpson was a secondary modern school and many of the girls were not academic and afraid of maths. Mother started to use her surveying experience to teach them at a time when practical maths was not taught in school. She started a Maths club which was very popular She wrote a pamphlet about this which caused a lot of interest and she was later asked to expand this into a book which was published by Hamish Hamilton in 1968. She was asked to appear on television in 'Tomorrow's World' on the BBC as her approach was so revolutionary.

In the early 1960s a new exam was being set up. This was the Certificate of Secondary Education (CSE). Before this the only school public exams were O (ordinary) level and A level and these were academic exams. Most people had no qualifications to show for their school years. The new exam expanded this with an overlap with O level – an A in CSE counted as a C in O level and was a pass (like a C in GCSE or a 4-5 now). Mother sat on the committee for the new exams and helped to shape the curriculum. The exam started in 1965.

In 1967 Mother became a lecturer at Coloma College, which was a Catholic teacher training college affiliated to London University. She was appointed Lecturer in the Institute of Education, London University and assigned to the Standing Sub-Committee in Mathematics. She continued with this until she retired.

After retirement Mother and Dad moved to Sandwich in Kent where she joined the local Bowls club. She became very good at this – she never did anything unless she was very good at it – and she became Captain of the Surrey County team.

Mother was an odd mixture and she changed substantially during my life. When I was small she was very tough and she felt (and I am sure was) very unloving towards me. She had very strong rules in some ways, although she did not police us at all when we were out of her sight. For instance Paul and I, and I think Mary, were not allowed ice cream or comics. One early memory is of managing to buy myself an ice cream and dropping some down my front. I can feel the complete panic I felt now as I tried to get the mark off so that she did not see. I would certainly have been smacked quite hard for that. Paul used to swap things at school for old comics and once she found a stash and burnt them. By the time the three youngest were reading not only were they allowed comics but they were put on the paper bill and delivered, and ice cream was a normal treat.

She was very generous with her time – Guide Captain, playing the organ in church, helping at a local children's home and others. She was also generous with my time, volunteering me to help. When I was a medical student I lived at home and she would beg the younger ones to 'Let Janet' help them, take them shopping, whatever. This was so common that it is still a saying between me and my siblings. She was also generous with money, although she did not have much. Things were quite tough when I was young and money very tight. She gave her things away and also mine, I lost a lot of favourite books. This last trait persisted and I remember Caroline resisting her trying to give a book to another grandchild, after giving it to Caroline for her birthday.

Mother and Dad used to have ferocious arguments, particularly at meal times. Dad's points tended to be intellectual but Mother's were emotionally based. She used to get emotionally involved with the problems of strangers while ignoring any her children might have.

Both parents put a high value on intelligence and academic success and they were very proud of their children's achievements. Their grandchildren were all clever too and as each one got to be a few months old Mother would say they were 'the brightest of the lot' (another sibling joke). I think my academic success contributed to her change in attitude to me – by the time I had my own children I think she loved me as much as the others and she was a very good Granny. In fact, both Mother and Dad, whatever their deficiencies as parents, were splendid grandparents.

Mother adored her two boys and made this very obvious. It is interesting that although both parents had favourites none of us resented either Paul and Stephen or Alison for this – we could see that it was our parents and not the child who were at fault and we were all always good friends.

That brings an end to Janet's written biography of the family. So we now move on to my story.

My birth to age 2

I was born on August 22nd 1950 the youngest child of Audrey and Allan Todd. At the time my older brothers and sisters were aged: Paul 11 ¾, Janet 10 ½, Mary 8 ½, Alison 2 ¾, and Stephen 1 ¾. An interesting story about my birth was told to me by your Great Granny, Audrey, when I was a grown up. She told me this and said she felt very ashamed, but I don't think it was anything to be ashamed of. At the time that Audrey got pregnant it was of course not a long time after WWII. Allan had joined up and during the war he rose to be a Captain in the anti-aircraft services. Obviously after the war there were loads of servicemen returning from the war and this is where Allan suffered a disadvantage. Everyone was saying you must employ all those young men who have gone off to fight. Allan had not, as such, fought and even worse he was not that young – he was 42 by the end of the war. So, he could not get a job for quite a time. This meant he and Audrey didn't have any money. Therefore, when Audrey became pregnant with me Allan panicked and he asked his brother, Jack, who was a doctor, if he had got any medicine to end the pregnancy. Jack gave Allan some pills and Allan gave them to Audrey. Audrey was going to take them, but then when it came to it she could not bring herself to do so, and she flushed them all down the toilet. So that is how come your Granny was born and therefore how come, eventually, you were born!

We, my parents, brothers and sisters lived in a house in Balham, London, until I was 2 years old. I obviously don't remember living there but I have heard two stories about me from that time. Our garden backed on to Wandsworth Common and we had bushes at the end of the garden. Apparently, once I was out of nappies, if I was out in the garden playing and I wet myself I would take off my pants and hang them on the bushes to dry. So everyone who walked on Common near our garden would see my pants. The other story is that one day I accidentally dropped a silver teaspoon down the loo. I didn't want to put my hand in the loo, so thinking I would be able to get it back I flushed the loo. All that happened, of course, is that I managed to flush the teaspoon away. I then made matters worse by dropping some more cutlery down the loo and flushing some more. I am not quite sure what on earth I was thinking, but that is what I did.

Another story I have been told is that I used to like collecting worms, and then putting them in my pocket. Occasionally Audrey forgot to check my pockets when she did the washing so when the washing came out there would be a heap of horrible slimy jellified worms in the clean washing. Yuk.

Age 2 - 4

When I was 2 years old the family moved to Merstham, originally to South Merstham. I do have some vague memories of my time there and once again I have been told a bit about our time there. I do recall two ladies, Miss Jakey and Miss Worzel, who lived in a big house on the corner of our street. At the time I did not understand it, but apparently they fostered or adopted quite a lot of children with disabilities. Because we were children of about the same age we would get invited round to tea quite often. In my memory they had a massive long table, like at school, but I don't suppose that it was really very big, just big to a small child. I certainly remember that often they had chocolate spread sandwiches, which I absolutely detested.

Another memory I have from this time is having pneumonia when I was four years old. I can remember one day sitting up in bed and playing with some paper cut out clothes which had flaps. You would use them to put on cardboard dolls. I suddenly felt very sick. Audrey had given me a bowl to be sick into, but I was sick all over the bed instead. The reason I did this was because my dolls clothes and cardboard dolls were in the sick bowl and I didn't want to ruin them. I also remember the doctor coming each day and giving me an injection of penicillin. He left the little glass bottles which contained the fluid behind and I collected them on the mantelpiece over the fireplace. However, somehow or other the bottles got knocked off the mantelpiece and smashed, and I was very upset about this. In this house I shared a bedroom with Alison and Stephen and one of us had a bed under the window. Outside the window there was a ledge and I can recall all three of us climbing on the bed and out of the window and sitting on the ledge. I should think Audrey and Allan would have had heart attacks if they had realised what we were doing.

A story I have been told about when we were living there, but I don't remember, was that I went to a nursery school and at this school had a friend called Lorna. A taxi used to come to pick Lorna up from school. One day, when we were leaving school, the taxi arrived and Lorna invited me to join her. The taxi driver must have been a bit of a clot as he allowed me to climb in as well and off we set. Then after a while Lorna told him to stop and the two of us got out. By this time I think the driver must have been completely bonkers, as he let two little 4 year old girls just wander off on their own. Of course when Audrey arrived to pick me up from nursery I wasn't there. The police were called and everyone was out looking for us. I don't think it took very long to find us, but poor Audrey must have been absolutely terrified as to what had happened. Apparently when we were found we were questioned as to what had happened but my reply was "I'm noggone tell you what me and Lorna done". I believe I never did tell anyone any more about that little escapade.

Primary school age

When I was about 4 ½ my grandparents, who had lived with us in South Merstham, and my parents decided that the house we were living in was much too small. By this time Allan had got a job, working as a journalist for the Financial Times newspaper. So, the grown-ups pooled all their money and we moved to a newly built house in what was called the village – a different part of Merstham. This was a big house and I lived in it until I left home. When we first moved in there was my grandparents, parents and 6 children. My granny died not long after we moved there and I don't really remember her at all. She suffered from dementia, so I think that was what made me a scared of her, the only thing I do remember about her. There was enough room for everyone to have a bedroom of their own, apart from myself and Alison. We shared a bedroom. Later on, as people left home, I first of all moved into Mary's room. This room was absolutely freezing cold in winter, as it was on the corner of the house, so had 2 outside walls, and it was over the garage. In those days we did not have central heating and there was often ice on the inside of the window. Later I moved into Janet's room, which was a bit, though not a lot, warmer. However, this probably explains why, to this day your Granny likes a cold bedroom with the window open.

Sharing a bedroom with Alison, as I did for a few years, was not the easiest thing to do. Alison used to get upset about things very easily and as I was younger than her she found it easy to vent her frustrations on me. One particular habit she had, when she was annoyed with me, was to grab hold of me, grab hold of my hair and swing my head against the wall with my hair. Another thing that used to happen was that she liked goldfish and we had a goldfish bowl in our room. However, the goldfish used to die with monotonous regularity. I would be fast asleep in my bed when I would suddenly be woken by Alison screaming at the top of her voice, because she would have found the latest goldfish floating dead in the bowl.

A story I have been told from before I started school is that Alison was being a superior sister and told me that she was much cleverer than me. I of course said she wasn't. So Alison said, 'ok, how do you spell 'the'?' As I had not started school I could not yet read or spell. So my reply was 'M A'. At this Alison scoffed and told me I was wrong. But I got the last laugh on Alison, as my response to that was 'I was spelling it in French.'

A very important person in my life moved in next door to us just after we moved to our new house. This was another Alison (Cullen), her parents and sister Elizabeth. Alison was just 5 months older than me and in fact we have stayed friends ever after. I am still in touch with her and we were supposed to be celebrating our 70th birthdays together in June. Because they were new houses, as they were being built people would move in before everything was quite finished and I expect even now there is my footprint on Alison's old front door step, because as soon as I heard someone was arriving I went round to her house and stepped in some still damp concrete. Alison and I were great friends right from the start and we used to spend much of our time round at each other's house, playing games. As far as I can recall we played a lot of games which involved being on horses. (Alison was fairly horse mad, and had riding lessons. I wasn't and have never had a riding lesson, but I still liked playing these games.) The horses were the corner of our beds, where we rode on exciting adventures.

We did not have a television, in fact I don't think we got one until I was about 8 years old, so another thing I liked about going to Alison's house was the chance of watching the tv, which was only in black and white, there was no colour tv back then. In those days originally there was just one channel, the BBC, and then in the mid 1950s ITV started. In the afternoon between about 4-6 there were programmes devoted to children. I can remember watching Andy Pandy, Bill and Ben and the Flowerpot Men, and Muffin the Mule in particular. If you go on the internet and find them you will think they are completely ridiculous and boring, but at the time it was all new and exciting. When we did get a tv they were very unreliable and the picture used to go round and round in circles a lot, or go very fuzzy. There were buttons to try and stop this on the tv, but generally hitting it hard on the side was a better method. At the end of the day, when the tv finished, which it did at around 10.30 in the evening, the National Anthem was always played and you were supposed to stand up to listen to it. As I got older I did stay up until the end of the tv, but I don't think anyone in the family ever even listened to the National Anthem, let alone stood up for it. The same thing happened if you went to the cinema, which we did very occasionally. At the end you were supposed to stand up and you did stand up but we, like most of the public, stood up in order to try and get out before they played the National Anthem.

Because there was very little choice with television viewing, some programmes became extremely popular and you would find that everyone was watching at the same time. I can remember cycling back from Brownies as fast as I could possibly go to get back in time for a science fiction series A for Andromeda. A later serial, The Forsyte Saga, was so popular that other events would be scheduled so that they did not clash with the time that it was being broadcast. There was no catch up tv or repeats, so if you missed an episode you missed it. There was also always a Sunday serial which was very popular and I can particularly remember watching A Tale of Two Cities with Allan, with the two of us passing a hanky between each other, drying our eyes from crying.

We did listen to the radio quite a lot, including a serial called Mrs Dale's Diary, which was hugely popular. In the evening, when he got home from work, Allan used to like listening to what was called the Third Progamme, which is nowadays Radio 3. This had, and still does have, classical music on it, so I was brought up listening largely to classical music, which probably explains why this is one of my passions to this day. We had what was called a record player for music as well. The first one I remember, you had to wind up before putting a record on. To make it work you had to pick up the arm with a needle and put it on the grooves of the record. Not surprisingly records were very easily scratched. I can remember the excitement when we got our first 'automatic' record player. You could play LPs, which could play music for about 30 minutes, then you would take the LP off and turn it over and play the other side. You could also play singles, which were much smaller and just had one song on each side, for a maximum length of 6 minutes. You could stack up to 10 of these on the spindle, and as each one finished the next one would drop down. This also led to quite a lot of scratches.

When I was 5 years old I started at school. My school, Merstham County Primary, was a fairly short walk away. You had to cross the main road going from London to Brighton to get to it. Although there was nothing like the amount of traffic on the road as there is today, because it was dangerous we had a lollipop man, who was extremely kind. His name was Mr Cox and he always kept humbugs in his pocket. He often used to give us kids humbugs when we crossed the road. The headteacher of the school I went to, Mr Agate, was a real character. During the 2nd World War he had done the most parachute jumps out of everyone and was in the Guinness Book of Records for this. He was great fun and I have several stories about him. One is that every Christmas we used to have a party, and Mr Agate, who was quite tall and big, always came to the party dressed up in fancy dress. There are two occasions when I can remember what he was wearing. Once he came dressed as a fairy, complete with a white tutu, a wand and a long blonde wig. The other time, and I think this one was the best of the lot, he came as a baby. Another member of staff pushed him into the room in a pram (I don't know how he got into it, perhaps it was especially built for him). He was dressed as a baby with a white frilly cap on his head, a dummy in his mouth, and the bit that the children liked best of all, a hole had been drilled in the pram and as he was pushed around a dribble of water, just like wee, came out of the pram.

Mr Agate liked to give children the chance to tell stories, so at Friday assembly a volunteer child would be chosen to tell the whole school a story they had made up. I used to love doing this and would regularly put my hand up, hoping to be chosen. I was chosen several times and I can remember climbing up what seemed like an immensely high step ladder and sitting at the top. Another thing Mr Agate did in the summer was to take all of the children in the school onto the playing field at the back of the school. No other teacher was there, just him. He would set up a cricket wicket and then anyone who wanted to bowl at him did. He would try and hit the ball into the air and all the children would try to catch him out. If you did manage to bowl him out you got 6d – which is sixpence in old money, worth 2 ½ p today, which bought a lot more than it does today – and if you caught him you got 1d. I remember one time I was the 'penny girl', which meant he had given me the bag with all the money in, ready to give out to bowlers or catchers. He hit the ball up in the air and it was coming down near me, so in my excitement I tossed the penny bag away, so I could catch the ball. All the money from the bag went all over the place.

Another thing Mr Agate did was to go into the playground with a huge great rope. He then stood and swung it round and round and the children had to jump over it. If they touched it they were out. One time when he did this I was one of the last 3 children left. When the bell went to restart lessons Mr Agate kept us 3 children back to carry on until there was winner. Sadly I did not win, I actually came 3rd, it was either Wendy Akehurst or Christine Woodhall who won. I remember this as Wendy and Christine were in the year above me and I did not like them, I thought they were bullies.

When I was in my last year at school, Mr Agate, as he did every year, took my year up to London to watch something called the Royal Tournament. I can't recall much about what happened in the show, which was a military show, though I do remember a lot of horses pulling gun carriages behind them. However, I do remember something extra special happening. After the show was over all the children were told to stay sitting in their seats as everyone else left. Then when the rest of the audience had gone, suddenly Mr Agate appeared, floating down from the very high ceiling on a parachute.

I don't remember anything much about being in the infant school bit of my school, but one story I have been told is this. The children were told to try and learn a poem or nursery rhyme. Janet, who loved poetry, decided to teach me one called Ye Spotted Snakes, from A Midsummer Night's Dream, which is written by Shakespeare. Apparently when I was going to school I said I was going to say: 'Poem by William Shakespeare. The other children won't know who he is, but the teacher will'. I think I was a bit of a bighead!

Once you were in the junior school the children were then split into 2 classes – the A stream and the B stream. Looking back it seems absolutely ridiculous. At the age of 7 you were assessed as either being more or less clever and depending on which you were meant to be you were in the A stream if clever and B stream if not. How daft is that? But sadly that is what happened then. I was in the A stream and in fact I used to be top of the class, along with Sandra Martin, for most of my time at the school. Generally speaking, unlike Grandad, therefore, I did very well at school. However, I did get in real trouble once when I was in 2A, what would now be year 4. We had a very chubby teacher, called Mrs Stribbling. I had gone home and written a rude poem about Mrs Stribbling, not because I didn't like her but because I thought it was funny. It was all about her dribbling and I can also remember it said that she went to the toilet and her poo went plop, plop, plop. Unfortunately, I took this poem into school and a boy, called Nicky Parsons, found it and went and put it onto Mrs Stribbling's desk. Obviously I got into trouble for this, but so did Nicky. We both had to go and see Mr Agate, which I obviously did not enjoy, and then I was sent down to class 1A for a week as punishment. However, I did a lot better than Nicky, as he was put in class 2B for a week. As I was put in a lower class, in which I had come top, I found the lessons very easy if work wasn't sent for me. However, the teacher of 2B, Mr Potter, was well known for being very lenient with the girls in his class and extremely strict with the boys. So poor Nicky had a miserable week.

Another exciting thing I remember from this school is that in winter, when it was very cold, we used to make a huge great ice slide in the playground and the aim was to get from one end of the slide to the other. I don't remember anyone falling and breaking any bones, although I expect it did happen occasionally.

A not so exciting thing, particularly in winter, was that the toilets were not in school, you had to go outside and walk right round the back of the school to get to them. We also did not have our lunch at the school, as the hall where we had assemblies was actually 3

classrooms, with sliding doors which opened and closed. So we all had to get into a great big crocodile and walk to the village hall for our lunch. We sat on tables of about 12 per table and the child at each end would be someone in the top year. They had to dish out the food, so you had to hope you got a nice child, not a greedy one who wanted to keep a large portion for themself. You had to eat everything you were given and teachers used to come round and check that you had done. I didn't like a lot of the puddings, so I would routinely give my pudding to someone else (which made me very popular, particularly when it was chocolate sponge with chocolate sauce) keeping a tiny bit to swirl around my plate, to make it look as if I had eaten it.

When I was in class 3A we had a horrible teacher called Miss Cox, who I remember had an oddly shaped sloping head and who everyone disliked. She was mean to the children and I particularly remember how she picked on a girl called Marilyn Tiller. Marilyn was left-handed, which in those days was very strongly discouraged. Anyway, the girls all had to make a skirt, which we had to hand sew. Because Marilyn was left-handed she sewed in a different direction to everyone else. Miss Cox got very cross with her and said she HAD to sew the 'right' way, which Marilyn didn't like. Eventually we all made our skirts and then she put them all in for display and a competition in the village show. Ha ha ha to Miss Cox, as Marilyn got first prize. Hooray. Miss Cox was mad keen on Scottish country dancing and all the girls were made to do this dancing. She then chose the best 8 girls for her team. I was one of the best 8, so I was in the team. The team consisted of 4 pairs, 1st boy and girl, 2nd boy and girl and so on. We were chosen for our parts according to our height, and I was therefore 3rd boy. We were entered for the All UK Scottish dancing championships and our team won. (Perhaps this is where Max and Harriet get their dancing skills from?) I still have a photo of me wearing my dancing dress with sash somewhere in the house. I am holding a cup, which I won for being sports girl of the year in my last year at school. Not only was I good at dancing, but I was also good at high jump and at swimming, where I won at the backstroke one year at a Surrey County inter-school competition. When I represented the County, however, I did not do well and went straight out in the heats.

At home, apart from playing with Alison C, I also played a lot with Stephen and Alison. Stephen used to be very interested in making things and he built ever more elaborate go karts, out of bits of wood, rope for steering and old wheels. We had a lovely time racing up and down the road in the go kart, but one day the go kart was sabotaged by Alan Goodchild (he certainly wasn't), a sneaky boy who lived round the corner from us. Stephen was enraged by this and he and I got our own back on Alan. One day we climbed up a tree. Then when Alan came past we pelted him with a big pile of mud balls, which we had taken up with us. He went home crying to his mum, who came round and complained about our behaviour to Audrey. She listened politely, but after Mrs Goodchild had gone simply commented what a silly woman she was to get involved in children's fights and no more was said about it.

It was Alison Cs uncle, Uncle Ted, who was the builder who built all the new houses on our road. As part of the planning permission, because the road backed on to a farmer's field, only bungalows could have gardens going down to the field, not houses. Alison lived in the last house before the bungalows and her uncle naughtily made sure that her garden did back on to the field. This was great for us children as it meant we could easily hop over her back fence and then we were off into the fields and woods behind. We used to roam for miles from our gardens, staying out playing all day in the woods and hills behind us. As we got a bit older we often used to set off on our bikes and ride for miles. We knew approximately when we were supposed to be home and the way that we were summoned back was that Audrey used to stand outside the door and ring a large bell. Once we heard that we knew we had to get back quickly. Sometimes the farmer kept cows in the field behind us and he would put up an electric fence to stop them from straying. Stephen used to think it was hilariously funny to make me touch the fence. I didn't. It didn't give a bad shock, of course, but it was certainly enough to be quite uncomfortable.

Because our house was one of the first to be built there were lots of builders around building the other houses and bungalows further up the road. The builders certainly didn't mind us playing around them so we did things that you would never be allowed to these days. The 2 Alisons, Stephen and myself used to have a lovely time playing on the sites and the builders used to give us rides on their dumper trucks. One builder always seemed to have a red jumper on, so we called him Robin Redbreast.

When the family went on holiday, because there was a lot of us, it was difficult to find anywhere big enough to take us all, but the solution was stay in converted railway coaches. The best year of the lot was the one when we went to stay at St Ives in Cornwall. That year was the one when I had my 5th birthday, I think at home but it could have been when we were on holiday. There are a number of things I remember from that holiday. The first is that there were no loos in the camping coaches, we had to go to the station and use the loos there. There was a lady who worked at the station, who we called the lavatory lady. She did not really like people to use the loos, as she wanted them to be permanently sparkling clean. So, she always had a vase of flowers in the loo and if you actually used one the minute you came out she would be in furiously cleaning it. One day my parents asked her whether she liked going to the beach out of the summer season, as it was a lovely sandy beach. She replied that she had NEVER been on the beach, she was far too busy cleaning the loos!

That summer Janet taught me to swim, in the sea. In those days no-one had anything like wet suits or anything, we children and adults alike just used to swim however cold it was, either in or out of the water. However, I was nearly always first person out of the sea as I was very skinny, just like Eddie, and I did feel the cold a lot when swimming. I used to emerge from the sea blue and shivering with cold. On the sand we used to make friends with other children on holiday and played lots of games with them, the most popular being French cricket. This was a game where whoever was in had a tennis racket and their legs were the wicket. The other children would then try and get them out by bowling a tennis ball at their legs, while the person in tried to hit the ball away. You were not allowed to change position, so if you hit the ball behind you accidentally it was difficult to avoid being out straight away.

The most exciting thing that happened on that holiday was fantastic and I have never heard of anyone else having such an amazing time. Because we were staying at the station we made friends with the 2 drivers of the steam train that used to do a regular shuttle between the main station at St Erth and the little local line that went to St Ives. So, the drivers used to take me, Alison and Stephen in the cab of the train. We would toot the horn, fill the train up with water and even shovel coal into the furnace. As we approached St Erth we had to duck right down so that no-one else saw us, as obviously we were not allowed to be in the cab. The drivers told us their names were Jack Robinson and Erroll Flynn, but I am sure that was not really their names. In those days if you talked about being quick you would say you were as quick as Jack Robinson. Erroll Flynn was an extremely famous film star at the time. However, I of course did not realise this and could not understand why people laughed when I told them the drivers' names.

On another year when we were holiday we went to stay in a camping coach in Tenby. That year a friend of Stephen's, Neil Yates, also came on holiday with us. One day a trip was planned to Pembroke castle. However, unfortunately, before we set off I was balancing on the railway lines, fell and cut my knee on a piece of corrugated iron. So the rest of the family went off to the castle and Audrey took me to the local hospital, where I had to have my knee stitched. (I still have a small scar on my knee, so it must have been quite a bad, deep cut.) I was upset at missing the trip to the castle, but matters were made even worse when they all got back, as Alison, Stephen and Neil were all giggling hysterically and taking me on one side they told me that whilst there they had locked some people in the dungeons. I was extremely jealous of them.

The other holiday I recall was the year we went to Highcliffe. That was a strange year as Audrey caught polio, which was an extremely serious illness, and had to go and stay in hospital. Luckily I was too young to understand how bad it was, but I did not like not having my mother around. We had booked this holiday, so Allan decided it would be good for all of us to go away. Before setting off he made some sandwiches to eat on the train. When it came to time for the sandwiches the older ones started eating and then asked what on earth was in them. Allan told them and they realised that he had made sandwiches using the dog meat.

At home, on one of the hills behind the house, there was a large patch of blackberry bushes and in season Audrey used to send all of us out to collect blackberries. We used to take saucepans and bowls and come back laden down with them. One time Neil Yates had come to stay. Stephen, Neil, Alison C and I went out blackberrying and the two boys thought it would be funny to smear blackberries all over Alison. Her mum was very cross about this, as she got blackberry juice all over her clothes. Stephen and Neil certainly got into trouble for doing this.

Neil was the son of Betty and Sid Yates who had lived in a flat in our house in Balham. After we left London Audrey and Betty kept in touch and one year not just Stephen but I, too, was invited to go and stay with the Yates. At the local cinema they showed a week-long serial of a Superman story. Alas Stephen and Neil managed to get themselves into trouble again, this time by doing something to me – I can't remember what. The reason I remember this happening is because the next day was the final episode of the Superman story. When the last episode I saw ended Superman and his friends were stuck down a mine, with boiling oil pouring towards them and there appeared to be no escape. As punishment for being horrible to me, Stephen and Neil were told they could not go to the last episode of Superman. But that meant I couldn't go either. So I never did find out how they escaped from the mine.

When he was quite young Stephen got a bit obsessed with lighting fires and whenever he managed to get hold of a box of matches he would find somewhere to light a fire. This was a dangerous thing to do, as for example he once lit a fire in a cupboard in his room. Audrey cured him of this habit by sending him out into the garden to light bonfires constantly, but before this happened Alison and I were with him when he lit another fire that could have been disastrous. Near our house was a very large abandoned house, Merstham Grange. We used to go and play in the grounds and found a way to sneak in the house, which was boarded up. One day we went down to the cellar and Stephen lit a fire down there. He could, of course, have set the whole building on fire, but luckily didn't. It never crossed mine or Alison's mind that we should stop him, or tell anyone what he had done.

Everybody had a milkman in those days, who would come round each day delivering the milk in glass pint bottles. I used to very much like our milkman and in the holidays and on Saturdays I would often get up early and join him on his milk float and help him by delivering the milk and collecting the money. I felt very grown up. Sometimes he would reward me with a bar of chocolate, which made it even better.

I don't know how old I was when we first got a car, I think I must have been about 10, but once we did if we were going out for the day the whole lot of us used to pile in. Audrey would drive the car and I sat in the front on Allan's lap, everyone else would be crammed in the back. In those days we did not have seat belts at all, not for anyone. If we came to a hill that was at all steep we all had to get out and walk up the hill, as the car, which was really only big enough for 4 people, could not cope with getting up it laden down with people. We had to carry lots of water in bottles in the boot, as the engine used to boil over from the car getting overheated. We would then have to stop, wait until the radiator had cooled down a bit, and then fill up with water before setting off again.

In the summer we often met my Uncle Jack and Aunty Dorothy and their 4 children David, Peter, Charles and Margaret (known as the Farnham Todds, as this is where they lived) for picnics. Peter, my favourite cousin, who is the same age as me, is possibly the most key person in this story, so you will hear more about him later. When we went on these picnics we were rather jealous of the Farnham Todds. My parents used to make brisket (which is a type of beef, which has been stewed and then squashed in a hand press) and lettuce sandwiches to eat, with fresh fruit to follow, and if we were lucky orange squash to drink, although it was often just plain water. However, the Farnhams would have pork pies, cheese triangles and crisps and Penguin biscuits, and had Tizer or lemonade to drink. As a grown up I know I would much prefer what we had, but as a child I would, of course, have preferred what they had. Interestingly as an adult my cousin David told Janet that they would have liked to have had our brisket and lettuce sandwiches.

At home in the evenings Allan often read to us children in the evening. The book I particularly remember him reading was The Lion, the Witch and the Wardrobe. I love that book to this day and if ever any of you want me to read it to you I will do so very happily. We had a coal fire in our living room and we kids (Alison, Stephen and myself, the others were too big) used to sit on the rug in front of the fire whilst Allan read to us. It was normal to have a coal fire but we were very upmarket, as instead of lighting the fire with newspaper and sticks we had a gas poker. You would switch on the gas and then light the poker with a match. There were holes all along the poker and flames burst out of these. Then the poker would go in the fireplace until the coal had lit.

The method of heating the water was by a coke boiler, which was in the kitchen. That had to be kept alight all the time, as if it went out we had no hot water. So even on boiling hot days in the middle of summer we had the boiler going. The coke was shovelled in through a lid at the top and the ash would drop through the grid at the bottom. Every day someone had to empty the ash out with a shovel and then it was usually spread on the garden. Outside the back door we had 3 outhouses, one for coal, one for coke and one for garden tools. The coal man would come round and deliver a ton of each, carrying 20 x 100 weight bags on his back.

About when I started school Audrey got a job as a teacher in a local secondary school. This meant there had to be someone at home when we got back from school. So we had a sort of Rebel. However, unfortunately, although she wasn't unpleasant, she was not a very nice person or even particularly interested in us children. She was just there to do a bit of housework and to cook us our tea before Audrey got back. She was an awful cook, so that at least partly explains why Alison and I took up cooking from a very early age. Another reason why we both liked cooking was because we used to get hauled off to church every Sunday by Audrey. None of us was interested in religion and found church very boring. However, we always had a big Sunday lunch. So, someone had to stay at home to cook it. That meant there were always volunteers to cook, as it meant getting out of church. I started cooking meals for 9 people from the age of about 8. When meals were served Allan used to carve the meat, then the plate would be passed up the table to Audrey, who served out the vegetables. We were always served in the 'right' order, which meant Grandad was first, then all the girls from oldest to youngest, then the boys (poor Stephen) and then Allan and Audrey. We always had a pudding as well, which was usually fresh or cooked fruit, usually squashed apple, or a pudding made from whipped Carnation milk and jelly, which was known as Balham blancmange, or Venetian soufflé, or Stink puff. The reason for the last name was because the jelly would be strawberry or raspberry, so the pudding was pink. This made a pudding of pink stuff, which then became stink puff. After the meal we all had to help clear the table and then the unlucky ones would have to do the washing up, drying up and putting away. I can remember often feeling very annoyed with Paul, as he was very vague and dreamy and he seemed to spend much of the time wandering round the table quoting poetry, rather than helping. However, Janet has told me that apparently Paul was very often the one who did the washing up. I don't remember this.

I mentioned the washing and worms when I was little, which I don't remember, but I do remember doing the washing. We had a big tub which we filled with a hose from the tap. Then the motor was switched on and the washing would churn in the tub. Once that was done we drained the water out by opening a tap on the side of the tub, and a fresh load of water was poured in for rinsing the clothes. Finally, to help the washing dry more quickly, the mangle would be brought out and everything would be squeezed through the mangle to try and get rid of as much water as possible. In a house of 9 it would have been very difficult to wash and dry all the sheets, so we used to send them off to the laundry. A van would come round every week picking up and dropping off sheets and pillowcases, which were always white, not just washed and dried, but freshly ironed as well. That is a luxury from those days that we don't get today.

Paul (and the other big ones) was a very kind big brother. He often had friends round to the house and there was one in particular that as a small child I fell in love with and announced I was going to marry. His name was Lance and he, too, was very kind to me and often carried me around on his shoulders, which I loved. If Paul's friends stayed the night, which they frequently did, in the morning I would cook them scrambled eggs for breakfast and they used to pay me. I did not get a lot of pocket money, the going rate was 1d for each year of your age, from 5 upwards and then at age 10 you got a whole shilling (now 5p). This was a jump as a shilling was 12d. That sounds like nothing, but of course money then was different and a shilling would buy you at least a comic and e.g. a Mars bar. I used to like getting comics, as I have always been a great reader, my favourites were Bunty and Judy. I also used to buy 'grown up' books in comic form. So that way I read a lot of books that you won't read until you are well into your teens.

I adored my Grandad, who lived with us until after I left home. He had his own room, it was called Grandad's study, and I spent a lot of time in there chatting to him. He was a very clever, interesting man who knew about all sorts of things, although he had left school at 14 and was almost entirely self-educated. He taught himself to read French and German and Latin, and he had an extensive library of books. I think I got my love of reading from him, as we would discuss books at great length. He was very fit and active and would go out for a walk every day. He also had a very heavy bicycle, with only 3 gears, and when he was in his late 80s cycled all the way from our house up to Durham, where Uncle Jack's twin sister, Joan, lived.

Secondary school

When I was in my final year at primary school all the children took the 11+, an exam which decided whether or not you went to the local secondary modern school or to grammar school. This was very important, as if you went to the grammar school you would be expected to take O Levels and probably A Levels, which meant you could go on to university or teacher training college. If you went to the secondary modern your choices were very limited and it was hard for children who went there to go on to do more academic subjects. There were many more places at the secondary moderns, only about 10% of children went to grammar school. In my school only 5 of us passed the 11+, and 2 of us, myself and Jennifer Williamson, who was my best friend at primary school, went on to Reigate County Grammar school for Girls. It was usual in those days for schools to be just for boys or just for girls. There was also a grammar school for boys in Reigate, but it was about half a mile away from the girls school.

The school was 3 miles away from our house, so I would catch the bus to and from school – I can remember the number of the bus, the 414. We did not have uniforms at primary school, but we did at the grammar. In winter we wore a white blouse, a green skirt and a navy jumper. Even though we were girls we also had to wear ties, which were striped green and navy. In summer we did not have to wear a tie, thank goodness. Summer and winter we had to wear a horrible green beret, which we were meant to wear all the time we were in uniform, so that meant we even had to wear it on the bus. Like everyone else I disliked wearing the beret and used to take it off the minute I got on the bus. However, one day a 6th form (year 12/13) prefect was on the bus and caught me not wearing my beret and reported me. I got an after-school detention and had to stay behind and write an essay on the topic of 'Why I should wear my beret'. This was difficult to write, as I could not think of a single good reason. However, I made up some reasons which I thought would please the teachers. But I was so cross that I spelt the word beret as berry (like e.g. a strawberry or raspberry) all through the essay. When I gave my essay in the teacher was very suspicious, as I was very good at spelling, but luckily accepted that I did not know how to spell beret properly.

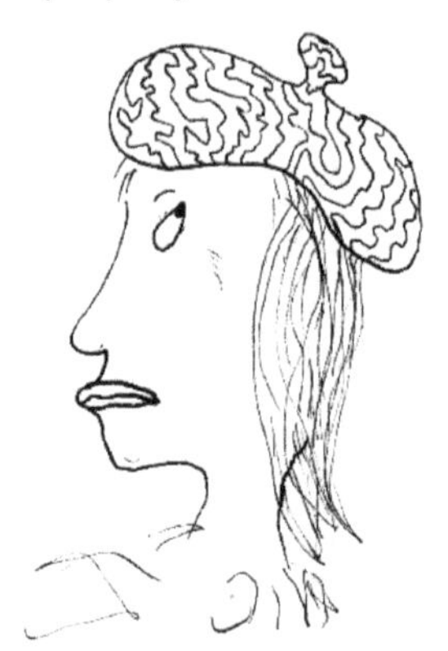

I have said at primary school I was top of the class. This did not continue at grammar school. I settled in to being about in the middle, neither very good nor very bad at anything, except at Art, at which I was atrocious. I had this confirmed to me by my art teacher, who I only had in my first term at the school. I think he was probably a supply teacher, as I never saw him again after that term. One time he gave us homework which was to paint a picture of our bedroom. When he gave the pictures back he would stop at some of them and hold them up to show the class something very good about the painting. The very last painting he came to was mine, which he held up for all to see. I was a bit puzzled by this, as I had long realised that art was certainly not something I was good at. But he didn't hold it up to show how good something was. I can remember to this day what he said about my work. He said: "This is a perfect example of everything that is wrong in a painting". It is a good job I found this funny, as someone else might have been very upset at being shown up in front of the rest of the class.

I enjoyed some lessons at school, but some I did not like at all and usually if I really disliked them I did pretty badly at them. We did not have a national curriculum and once you reached year 10 you had to choose subjects to do for O Levels. I was very disappointed at how the school arranged things, as unless you did all 3 sciences as separate subjects you had to choose to do either biology, or physics with chemistry. I was good at physics and wanted to do it. But of course I couldn't do just physics. Sadly whoever taught us chemistry was a rotten teacher and I had absolutely no idea what on earth was going on in chemistry. I was therefore forced to choose to do biology. Ever after I have regretted this, because it has meant I am scientifically illiterate as a grown up. Grandad talks to me about all sorts of interesting scientific things and I wish I understood them better.

However, I really enjoyed music, history and English, which I chose to study when I did my A levels. I also liked maths and geography and I enjoyed doing sport as well. We did hockey, gym and netball in the winter and spring terms, and rounders, athletics and tennis in the summer term. We did swimming all year round. I was a reasonable player at everything and I was in the school teams for everything apart from tennis.

My best friend at secondary school was called Claire Duncan, but right from the start she was called Chips. (The reason she was called that was because when she was born her Dad had said she was 'a chip off the old block' and the name Chips stuck.) Because Chips and I were best friends and because we girls liked giving each other nicknames, I acquired the nickname of Fish. As I got older I and my friends made friends with the boys at the grammar school and a lot of days instead of just getting the bus and going home a crowd of us used to meet at Pearl's café, where we would sit and chat for ages. I don't know what Pearl thought of this, as we only ever bought one coffee or tea each and hardly ever bought any cakes, so we took up her café yet spent hardly any money.

At the weekends there was nearly always a dance at a hall in Reigate, where there was always a live band. It would be exciting to say that I first saw a band perform there which later became famous, but I didn't. I don't think any band ever did anything other than play at little places like this. However, through Alison, I did get to know someone whose brother was in a very famous group. Alison went to a college for her A Levels, where her particular friend was Bronwen. We saw a lot of Bronwen and in time, when Bronwen started dating, and went on to marry Frank Lynes, we saw a lot of Frank as well. Frank's brother, Roy, became a member of the pop group Status Quo. If you look them up on the internet you will easily find them. I didn't really know Roy, but I certainly met him.

However, when I got a little bit older, another place I would go to was the Redhill folk club, usually with Alison. It was held in the back room of a pub (which is why I had to be a bit older, as children were not allowed into pubs in the evening) and was only a small venue. There were some people who visited there who later became famous. The one I most remember, and even remember one particular song he sang, was a man called Bert Jansch. He came on his own but later was part of a famous group called Pentangle. The song I remember him performing was called 'The Needle of Death'. This was an anti-drugs song, the message being if you took drugs you could kill yourself. I don't recall drug abuse being particularly high in the 60s, but it just goes to show that it was already causing problems.

During my teenage years I started dating boys. I never had a boyfriend for very long and neither did my friends. We all swapped around with the boys we were friends with. I had the added advantage that Stephen went to a different grammar school in Purley, so I also had boyfriends from his group of friends. I was very keen on just one boy, Geoff Evans, who was very good looking and tall and an excellent sportsman. He was the star of both his football and cricket teams and later went on to play cricket for Surrey. I used to like being the girlfriend of the star player. However, sadly he ditched me after about 5 months (which for me was a very long time for a boyfriend).

It was not a regular thing to eat out and not even to have a takeaway. Although we had fish and chips, this was cooked at home and always on a Friday. We used to have a big pan of oil with a basket to cook the chips in. These chip pans were actually very dangerous and sadly quite a lot of people were killed in house fires or were badly burned by spilling oil, but they were very common. I am glad to say nothing ever happened to any of us. The first exciting meal out I remember was for Alison C's 16th birthday. Her parents took us to a Chinese restaurant, which was newly opened in Reigate. I had never had Chinese food before and found it very exotic.

Another thing that was dangerous, although at the time we thought nothing of it, was that Alison, Stephen and myself plus friends used to go swimming in a disused quarry near Redhill. We would set off with our swimming things and a picnic, and catch a bus to near the quarry. We would then spend the day there. The quarry was extremely deep and extremely cold but we used to love going there.

As I got a bit older it was perfectly normal to hitch hike, everybody did it. You would stand by the side of the road and hold your thumb out. A driver would then stop and give you a lift. If they were not going as far as where you wanted to get you simply hopped out the car and started hitching again. Our nearest seaside town was Brighton so if I wanted to go to Brighton for the day, that was how I got there and back. There was a train that went from Merstham to Brighton but I could not have afforded to catch a train. At the weekend Stephen and I quite often used to hitch hike to Purley, where most of his friends lived, and meet them in a pub. Some of them had access to cars and after the pub people did not go home but went round to someone's house and stayed out until 1.00 or 2.00 in the morning. Luckily the usual meeting place was at our house. We would get a lift back with someone and then we all sat around having some drink, playing cards and chatting.

Post school and on to university

Whilst I was at school I applied to university to do Politics. However, probably because I was stupidly rather lazy about doing my revision, although I did well at English A level, I did not do very well at either History or Music. This meant I did not get into university. This left me with a problem. Having heard from my elder siblings what fun it was, I was really keen to go, but I certainly did not want to go back to school to retake my A levels. I therefore enrolled at a college, intending to redo History and to take another A level (I can't remember what). However, fortunately Janet's husband, Peter, spoke to me and said he thought I would enjoy doing law. He said if I did that I could enrol at one of the Inns of Court and go and study law, without having to get better A levels. I don't know why I hadn't thought of doing law before, which I hadn't, in view of the fact that three of my siblings, Paul, Mary and Stephen had all done law. I often think I was a bit silly. Anyway, I thought that was an excellent idea, left the college and enrolled at Grays Inn.

Grays Inn is in London and I did not want to commute from Merstham on the train, I felt I was old enough to leave home. Luckily for me Audrey and Allan had not sold our old house in Balham, but had had it converted into flats. One of the flats, right at the top where the Yates' used to live, was vacant so I moved in there. I liked studying law right from the start and made a number of friends. However, I did not like living in London and I didn't like the way at the end of the day or evening everyone just disappeared off to their homes, which could be miles apart. So I decided to reapply to university, but this time to do law.

Of the 6 universities that I applied to 5 of them simply rejected me. However, very fortunately for me, Newcastle university asked me to go for an interview. When I got there I was given a test, to see if I had the right aptitude for law. This was even more fortunate, as when I went in for my interview the interviewers, having asked me what I was studying, said, 'Oh, that explains why you gave the answer you did'. I had given the correct legal answer to a question, which others who had not studied any law would not have done. As I was leaving they told me that I would hear in about the next 2 weeks as to whether I had got in, but as I was walking out of the department someone came running up to me to ask me to go back for a minute. When I did the interviewers said they had decided to take a chance on me and I could go. I was absolutely thrilled about this, particularly as Alison C was already there, having got a place the previous year. I was warned that they would be keeping a close eye on me, as my A levels really were not good enough for me to have a place.

I had a brilliant time at university, I loved it all. I made some really good friends, one of whom, Gill Matthews, is godmother to Anna (and whom I saw recently). Another of my very good friends, George Connell, was a particularly useful friend to have, as he had a car. In those days not many students had their own cars and even if they did they were not allowed to bring them to university. However, George had had an operation on his back, so he was medically allowed to bring his car. This meant that we could travel around in his Morris Minor estate, a rather strange looking car with struts of wood on the outside, in a way that other students couldn't.

I think it was probably George who first made me realise that I would like to be a law academic. He was very bad at one particular subject, Land Law, which was a subject I enjoyed and was very good at. So I spent quite a lot of time tutoring George, so that in the end he did well when it came to the exams. I felt as pleased with his exam result as I did with mine. As I enjoyed law I worked hard at it, which is more than can be said for several of my friends. Working hard certainly paid off, as at the end of my 2nd and 3rd year, when I took exams which counted towards my final degree, I came top of my year both times.

It was at university that I had the first Indian meal I had ever had. A crowd of us went out with one of my friends, Nuala, and her boyfriend (later husband) Bren, to an Indian restaurant. No-one, apart from Bren, had ever been to an Indian restaurant before. So we all relied on Bren to order the food, as none of us knew what anything was and didn't know what to ask for.

A big feature of the university year was Rag week. This was a week where all sorts of events went on, a lot of them silly, to raise money for charity. I especially remember being in the Rag band, which involved parading through town, dressed in night things, women in men's pyjamas and men in women's nightdresses. Everyone brought an 'instrument' with them, which they played. I had a kazoo, other people had pots and pans, combs with tissue paper, bicycle bells and lots of other daft things.

University was also a time when a lot of young people would get together to protest about whatever was the big issue of the day. Whilst I was there an MP called Margaret Thatcher, who would later become our Prime Minister, was Minister in charge of education. At school every child would get a free bottle of milk a day to drink, a small third of a pint bottle. This was because during and after WWII there was rationing of many foods, including milk and cheese and children were not getting the necessary vitamins and minerals needed. I certainly remember those bottles, as the milk was often horrible. This was because we either had it straight from outside and then it was often frozen, or if it had been brought in it was put by the radiators and was luke warm. Margaret Thatcher had decided that children did not need milk any more, as it was now a long, long time after the war and children were now well fed. However, there was (and still is) a lot of poverty, and many people thought that it was vital to carry on giving children milk. There was a big protest meeting at the university, which I went on, and we marched through the streets waving banners and shouting 'Margaret Thatcher, milk snatcher'. We ended up with a rally in a cinema building. Shortly after we had all piled in we got a message that a bomb threat had been sent to the cinema, and we should all leave. But no-one would budge, and of course there wasn't a bomb.

The Law Department was on the 10th floor of an 11 floor building. To get lots of students up and down this tower all at the same time would have been very difficult unless there were a lot of lifts, which there weren't. However, what the tower did have was a paternoster. This is a no door, constantly moving lift which just goes round and round in a circle and which will take 2 people at a time. So you stepped on at the bottom and off when you got to the floor you wanted. You could simply stay on and go over the top or under the bottom, which was quite fun as you could see the workings of the paternoster. What you will find amazing is on the way up you could see that the whole of the 3rd floor of the building was taken up by the university computer. That was it, there was no other computer of any kind in the rest of the whole of the university! We had no internet, no mobile phones or anything like that.

At university I again had quite a lot of boyfriends, but only one that I really liked and who ended up ditching me. (This is beginning to sound like a pattern.) His name was Paul Fuschillo, who, like the other boyfriend I had been keen, on was very handsome. He was the star of the university football team. However, I never got to see him play, as he was very superstitious, because the one time a girlfriend of his had been to watch him play he broke his leg. After he left university he went on to be bought by a very famous manager, Brian Clough, and played in what was then called the 1st division (now the premiership) for Brighton. But he didn't last long, as he got injured and had to retire.

Post university

In my final year at university I had decided I definitely did not want to become a solicitor or a barrister and that I did want to become a university lecturer. I was working on drawing up a proposal for research when my Head of School, Bill Elliott, called me in to his office. He had had a phone call from one of his friends, Brian Hogan at Leeds University. They were looking for a young lecturer to take up a post for a year, as one of their members of staff was going abroad for a year and they needed a temporary replacement. Bill Elliott had suggested me and told me I was to go to Leeds for an interview. My interview consisted of Brian Hogan sitting in his room, with his feet up on his desk, asking me what subjects I thought I could teach. (When you grow up you will find that nowadays this never, ever happens. Another thing that never now happens is to go straight from an undergraduate degree to a university lectureship. Nowadays you always need a postgraduate degree.)

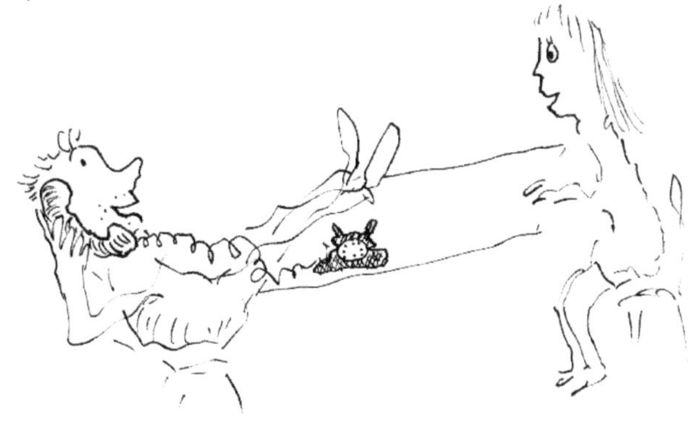

I had a great year teaching at Leeds. I was basically the same age as, or even younger than, many of the students, and although I was friends with other members of staff, most of my friends were students. There was one particular teaching incident that stood out in that year. For some rather odd reason which I never understood, when putting students into tutorial groups of about 6 people, someone decided that it would be a good idea to put all the troublesome, idle students in the same group. That was bad enough, but then they assigned me as one of the tutors for this group. These students did not prepare the work they were set and in about the 3rd week that I was teaching them, when they came in one of the boys sat down and started reading a newspaper. When I asked him what he thought he was doing he very rudely replied 'I am reading about the home life of our own, dear, Queen'. The others in the group giggled and looked delighted. At that I picked up the phone on my desk and rang through to the Dean of the department. I told him I was sending a group of students to see him and sent them off. After that the group was disbanded and I never experienced any more trouble from any of my students.

The next job I was appointed to was in Sheffield. I had a proper interview for this one. I was thrilled to be going there, as my sister Mary was already a lecturer there in the law department. I spent the rest of my working life in the Sheffield department, apart from the 2 years that Grandad and I spent in Canada, which I am coming to shortly. My year at Leeds had shown me that lecturing was the job I wanted to do. I enjoyed all aspects of the job. I liked the students and they (largely, I presume some didn't) liked me. I was quite happy to do various administrative tasks and once I got going, I enjoyed researching and writing.

When I first moved to Sheffield I lived with Mary and her husband, Mike, and their then 3 children (they later had 2 more). This was only a temporary situation and I bought my first house soon after arriving, which cost me £4,500. It was a terraced house in Crookesmoor, near the university, with 2 downstairs rooms, 2 first floor bedrooms, one tiny, a bathroom and an attic conversion. There was also a very small patch of garden at the back, with an outdoor loo at the bottom of it. All the time I lived in that house I had friends living with me as tenants.

Grandad and I

It was while living in my house in Crookesmoor that I met Grandad. This is the story of how I met him. My favourite cousin Peter was a doctor. He rang me up and said he was back from working in Zambia, which he had been doing for 2 years, and he would like to come and see me. Of course I was delighted to be seeing Peter. On the phone he also said that he knew someone working at Sheffield Children's Hospital, who he'd been friends with in Zambia. This, of course, was Grandad. I actually slightly misunderstood the conversation, as I thought that the 2 of them had been special friends in Zambia, whereas in fact they had only overlapped by 3 months and although friendly with each other, they were certainly not special friends. Because of this misunderstanding I therefore thought it would be nice for the 2 of them to meet up. So I rang the hospital and asked to speak to Grandad. When he came on the phone I said to him that he would not know me, but my cousin was Peter Todd. When I said that there was a long pause and Grandad said 'Who?'. I thought I had got the wrong person, but when I said Peter worked in Zambia Grandad realised who I was talking about. So Grandad said he would love to come round to see Peter. I did think that Grandad might be an interesting person to meet, perhaps to be a boyfriend, but my very first impression of him was to think 'No, not him'. Grandad looked very scruffy and had a horrible brown anorak on. However, by the end of the evening I had changed my mind about him, as I found him to be very interesting and very funny.

After that we met once or twice when Grandad had a party at his flat and when he invited me to a party at the hospital and then he asked me on a proper date. He invited me round to his flat and said he was going to cook a meal. This meal was revolting. He had bought some packet mix for bread, which he made. He had obviously put far too much water in and it was like trying to eat a brick. He also cooked steak, potato and cabbage, all of which he put on at the same time and left to cook for 45 minutes. Ugh, it was horrible. As I was trying to be polite I ate all the food on my plate, but Grandad just took one bite of each, laughed and gave up.

Grandad and I very quickly realised that this was more than just a casual relationship. I had arranged to go abroad to Australia for a year and the date was looming for me to book my flight, but I told Grandad and he suggested I didn't go. 10 days after the disastrous meal we decided to go to Cambridge for the weekend. There I got the most romantic proposal you could hope for. We went out in the evening to a little Italian restaurant. We sat in a booth, with a candle on the table and soft lighting. Everything was perfect for this romantic proposal. What actually happened was that Grandad said to me "Well I suppose we might as well get married then." I hope you grandchildren manage a rather better proposal than that.

I rang Audrey and Allan to tell them I had got engaged, which they were a bit surprised by. As they had not even heard of Grandad before, this is not surprising. Not long after that they came up to Sheffield to visit us and I am glad to say that they both got on extremely well with Grandad right from first meeting him. The same cannot be said about Grandad's parents. We decided to go down to visit them in Brockenhurst, where they lived. Annie, Grandad's mum, was always a bit strange and she certainly did not take to me. I was not a Catholic and I was 'too clever by half' was her view. So I am afraid the atmosphere was rather tense and we had to escape early. Eventually I think she sort of came round to me, but I don't think we ever really got on well, which was such a shame as I certainly wanted to.

When I rang Peter to tell him we were getting married he was very surprised, because, as I have said, he and Grandad didn't really know each other that well. However, he was obviously delighted. It is strange that it was Peter who introduced me to my future husband, because when we were little Peter and I decided that when we got older we were going to marry each other.

We got married on September 3rd 1977. It was a lovely day and I (not surprisingly) thought we had a lovely wedding. My dress was made by a friend, Sheila, who had been at the meal when I first met Grandad. The bridesmaids were all my nieces who were born at the time, plus Grandad's sister, Mary. Their dresses were all made either by their Mums or by a dressmaker. The reception was held in the garden and house of my sister Mary and Stephen's parents-in-law did all the catering. So as you can tell it was a very 'home-made' wedding. Grandad did not buy a new suit for the wedding, but when he had been in Zambia he had had a suit made for him, so he wore that. The day before the wedding he showed me the shirt he was planning on wearing, which was also not new (this is all typical Grandad). As it was rather crumpled I ironed it for him. However, when he left in the afternoon what did he do? He took the shirt and chucked it in a crumpled heap in the back of his car. It was at this point I decided that I was definitely not going to waste my time ironing his clothes when we got married.

Claire was born the following year on May 7th 1978, 2 days after I finished work at Sheffield. This was fairly amazing as our very first date had been on May 8th 1977. When she was born, as we were going to the hospital the only thing I could think about was what were we going to call her. For some reason we both thought she was going to be a boy and we could not decide what to call her. Grandad particularly liked the name Thomas and I liked the name Daniel. Both liked each other's choice but we couldn't decide which to choose. We had therefore decided on a compromise of Michael. I have no idea why, and as we were driving down I said to Grandad I definitely did NOT want the name Michael. We had settled on Claire for a girl, so that was easy. However, a lovely nurse came in and asked us what we were going to call her. We said Claire. She responded that you don't call a child Claire, you call them Claire Louise. So that is what she became.

Canada

6 weeks after Claire was born we moved to Canada. Grandad had got a job in a hospital in Kingston, Ontario and I was quite happy to take time off work and look after our new baby. One excellent thing Claire did, quite how I really do not know, was to immediately adjust to the time difference. When we landed in Canada, we arrived in Toronto, and stayed the night with someone from Sheffield law department who, like me, was spending time in Canada. Claire, who was a very good sleeper almost from day 1, somehow or other on the very first night had an immensely long sleep, so right from the start she was awake during the day and asleep at night. When you are parents you will realise how brilliant that is.

In our first year in Canada we lived in some flats outside town, near a shopping mall. As Grandad was on call he sometimes had to get up in the middle of the night and drive through the snow to get to work. In the day he would often cycle to work in temperatures well below freezing. I had a rule that I would take Claire out for a walk if the temperature did not drop below -12 degrees Fahrenheit/-24 degrees centigrade. It was quite lucky if there was snow, because if I took her out for a walk on other days she would spend much of her time picking up stones to take home.

One quite scary thing happened whilst we lived in the flats. I had been shopping in the car, leaving Grandad and Claire at home, and when I got back there were some policemen in the car park. Someone had reported seeing a brown car driving into another car in the car park and then driving off. The car we owned was brown. So, the policemen came over and insisted I got into the back of their car. They then accused me of being the driver who had driven into the other car. I kept insisting I didn't but they would not take any notice. It took ages, but eventually they let me go, but not until after they had threatened to take me down to the police station.

I cannot remember how we met them, but during the first year Grandad and I met a couple, one of whom, Bev, was a lecturer in the law department at Kingston University. This turned out to be a surprise bonus for me, because the following September, out of the blue, I got a phone call from the law department. Right at the last minute someone had become ill and they did not have anyone to teach Family Law, so would I be interested? So, I did some teaching for a semester, which I really enjoyed. Canadian family law is based on English law but of course it has changed over time and I learnt a lot about Canadian family law.

After a year spent in the flat Grandad and I decided we would rather be in a house nearer town and the hospital, so we rented a house from a couple who were going abroad for a year. Because it got so cold in winter, the houses and flats were very well insulated and this particular house had triple glazing on the front door. One day, when Claire was about 18 months old and after Grandad had gone to work, I popped outside the front door to put the dustbin out. As I did so Claire was standing by the door and I could suddenly see she was going to push the door shut. I shouted 'No' and rushed back, but was too late. The door closed. It was on a yale lock, which meant I could not open it. Claire stood inside the house and as I did not come in she started screaming for me. I was now in a real panic not knowing what to do. Fortunately, we had made friends with some people just up the road, so I rushed up to them to see if they could help. They gave me an axe and I went back to the house. Then I called to Claire through the letter box to go and get her favourite doggy and as soon as she had moved away from the door I managed to smash the glass in the door with the axe. Then I could put my hand through the hole and reach the lock to open the door.

It was whilst we were living in this house that Anna was born. I did not see this but Grandad told me that when he was first bringing Claire to visit in the hospital Claire spent the whole time walking down to the hospital saying 'Bayben Anna' very happily. Unfortunately, when she and Grandad got into the lift at the hospital someone pushed the buttons on the lift, which upset her as she wanted to push them. So, she decided to have a temper tantrum in the lift and when the lift doors opened flung herself out of the lift, onto the floor, sobbing.

The summer before this, Mary's son Peter came to visit us in Canada. You will hear more of this Peter later. So, I left Grandad at home looking after Claire and set off in the car to pick him up at the airport in Toronto. Unfortunately, on the way the car broke down and this is when I had another adventure, which looking back on makes me shiver. I was standing by the side of the road, not quite knowing what to do, as in those days we did not have mobile phones. However, a car drew up with two men inside. They said they could fix the car and to get in whilst they went to fetch whatever tools they needed. I did not have much choice and did so. We then drove off to a rather ramshackle farmhouse, in the middle of nowhere, where they got the tools, took me back and fixed the car. Looking back I find this scary, as to get in a car with 2 strange men, in the middle of nowhere, is not a safe thing to do.

Peter had a lovely time staying with us but when he left he left us with a problem. He was going through a phase of loving stuffed animals and birds. He had a collection of them at home. One day, just before he went home, he went out on his own and came back carrying a stuffed moose head! He wanted to take it back to England with him, but obviously could not put it in his luggage. He therefore wanted us to arrange to send it to him. We did make some enquiries as to whether this was possible, but got the answer no, so we were stuck with a moose head in the house. I cannot quite remember what we did with it, probably put it in the nearest available dustbin.

Grandad had travelled back to England for an interview for a job in Chesterfield whilst we lived in the house, which he did not get, but he also became aware that there was a job going in Worksop. So he visited Worksop to see what he thought of it and very much liked it. He therefore applied for that job and was successful in getting it. The difficulty this made for us was that it was expensive to fly to and from England, so we had very little money. We therefore lived on a very restricted diet for a while. This did not bother Claire, who would have been perfectly happy to live on a diet of tomatoes "matoes" and cucumber "doodah". She was an absolute pest wanting these, so any meal we had we had to pass them to each other under the table, so that she would not see them until after she had eaten some of the other food.

Worksop

We arrived back in England in July 1980 and Grandad took up his new job, which was very hard work. He was the only consultant paediatrician and all his junior doctors were very junior doctors, most of whom did not want to specialise in paediatrics, but wanted to become GPs. This meant he was on call the whole time. Theoretically he was on a rota with doctors in Doncaster, but as it would take far too long for those doctors to get to Worksop in any sort of emergency, he was the person that the juniors used to call, regardless of who was meant to be on call.

When we first moved to Worksop we lived in a different house from the one we do now. It was at the top of Highland Grove. It was while buying this house that Claire managed to embarrass me in a spectacular way. We had gone to visit the house, which was being sold by an elderly lady. As we sat in the sitting room, having tea and cake, Claire decided to lie on the floor, underneath a small table, and to kick the table legs. I very quietly hissed at her to stop it, but she took no notice. So I hissed a bit louder. At which point she responded by saying, in a very loud voice, 'Please don't beat me Mummy". There was nothing I could say that would make it any better.

I went back to work at Sheffield University in August 1980. I was rung up by a former colleague, who told me that they just needed someone to cover for a year, whilst someone was on sabbatical and would I be interested in the job. We hired someone called Gill to help looking after Claire and Anna and she was the one who gave the nickname of Roo to Anna. She used to call her 'Anna spanner roo', which got shortened to Roo and the name stuck. Gill did not stay with us for very long, as she left because she was pregnant. She did not think that I was a very good cleaner (which I wasn't) and wanted someone better to help with the cleaning. She therefore told us about Rebel and that is how Rebel started coming to our house. One day, not long after Gill had left, at the time temporarily, I was out in the garden with Claire and Anna and mentioned to them that I should really be at work, but couldn't be as I needed to look after them. Rebel overheard this and said she would be happy to look after them whilst Gill was away. So Rebel took over looking after Claire and Anna, and in due course Sarah and Rachel as well, as Gill never came back. Of course Rebel has stayed with us to this day.

When Anna was very little she was extremely good at talking, she started saying recognisable words when she was only 9 months old. However, walking was not her strong point. She basically refused to let go of a helping hand and if I did manage to take my hand away she would promptly sit down. It got to the stage that if you gave her a piece of string to hold she could walk, even though it was entirely loose and of no support, but take it away and down she sat.

When I got pregnant with Sarah one of Grandad's colleagues, VP, who was an obstetrician, wanted to be my consultant obstetrician and wanted me to go and see him with the private patients, but not pay. This I did not want to do, nor did Grandad, and I did not like him anyway. So, I had to make up an excuse about why I could not possibly see him. Luckily I think he might have taken offence, as we never again got invited to one of his ghastly parties after that. I also managed to upset the person who was my consultant, Tom Cochrane, as when Sarah was born the normal practice was that women stayed in hospital for 2 days after the birth. However, I didn't want to stay and couldn't see any good reason for doing so, so I discharged myself against medical advice. Grandad, of course, agreed with me.

When Claire and Anna came to see me in the hospital just after Sarah was born, Claire was very excited and wanted to keep poking at Sarah and climb up on the bed. Anna wanted to see Sarah but she was just frightened by it all. Very briefly, for about 2 hours, Sarah was called Sally. The reason for this was that Grandad and I had 2 favourite names, Sarah and Rachel. However, we couldn't decide which one to choose, as Grandad slightly preferred Sarah and I slightly preferred Rachel. Sally was our compromise. However, after 2 hours I thought we were both being silly, so I said we should call her Sarah. That made it very easy when Rachel was born, we knew immediately what she was going to be called.

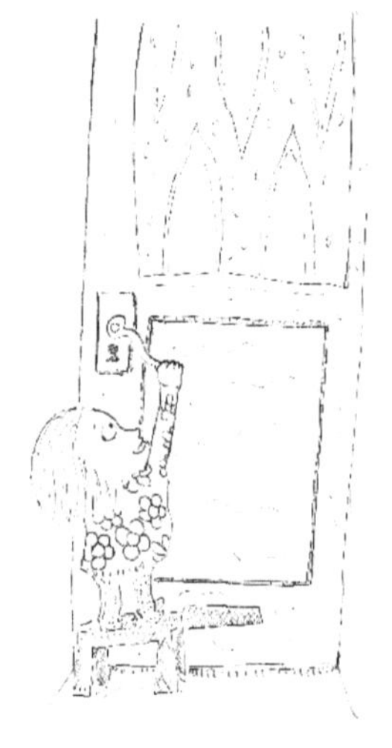

You have all probably heard the famous story of when Sarah was about 18 months old, but I will tell it here anyway. Grandad had gone to work. Claire was at school and Anna at nursery. I was in the kitchen, doing the washing up and Sarah wandered off to play. After a while, thinking it was very quiet, I called for Sarah. There was no answer. So I started looking for her. She was nowhere to be found. Then I realised that the front door was very slightly open. I then realised, aghast, that she must somehow have got out of the house. I rushed out of the house shouting for her. The major problem was she could have gone one of two ways. Either down the road, or on the path by the house next door, to the hospital grounds. I rushed over to our friend Janet Terry's house over the road and Janet, who was still in her dressing gown, said she would run down the road, while I went towards the hospital. So off I ran shouting her name all the time. As I got into the car park a lorry driver stopped me. He asked me if I was looking for a little girl. I said yes. He then said he had been driving through the car park and had seen a little girl wandering across it. So he had stopped and taken her into the nearest building, which was the maternity unit. I rushed in and sure enough there was Sarah, perfectly happy, playing with one of the nurses. Apparently when she had been brought in, the staff had rung through to paediatrics, where of course Grandad was working, to ask if they were missing any children. That, as you may know, was not the end of the story. The next day, when Grandad was also at home, the two of us hid out of the way and watched what Sarah did. She went into the downstairs loo, got the step for getting on the loo, and took it to the front door. She then climbed up on it, so she could reach the handle on the door, opened the door, and then set off down the garden path. As she went she was chattering very contentedly, saying 'No shoes, no shoes' as she did not have shoes on.

Rachel's birth was a bit too exciting for me. On the morning that she was born I woke Grandad up at about 6.00 and told him that Rachel was going to be born shortly and we needed to think about going into hospital. To which Grandad responded that it was far too early yet, turned over and went back to sleep. About an hour later I knew there was really not long until Rachel was born, so I woke up Grandad again and said he HAD to listen and we needed to get over to the hospital. This time he did listen, so he said he would go downstairs and ring Rebel, who had said she would come to be in the house to look after the older 3. Unknown to me, when he rang Rebel he said to her to come round – but told her there was no rush. By about 7.50 I was desperate and insisted we must go in, even though, to my surprise (as I did not know about the no rush comment), Rebel had not arrived. So Grandad came with me just to deliver me to the hospital door, which only took a couple of minutes, and then rushed back home as he'd left the other 3 in the house alone. Luckily Rebel then arrived and he came back to the hospital. 5 minutes later Rachel was born.

One incident that really stands out shortly after Rachel was born was one when I was out with her and the other 3. An old lady stopped me to admire Rachel lying in her pram. She asked me whether Rachel was a girl or a boy and when I replied girl she responded by saying “you must be so disappointed”. I am not sure I have ever felt so angry in my life as when she said that. Disappointed? In my gorgeous 4th daughter? How dare she?!

Life once we had all 4 girls

Generally speaking my work life was not very eventful. After the one year when I was filling in for an absence, another colleague wanted to go from being full time to part time, so we ended up splitting her job and both of us worked half time. I stayed half time for the rest of my career. I taught various different subjects over the years but my greatest love was Family Law and over the years I specialised more and more in that subject. Grandad's and my job overlapped slightly, in that an area of interest for me was child protection, and of course he was dealing with children who needed protection, as a paediatrician. This led to a couple of quite funny incidents. One year I was invited to give a guest lecture at King's College, Cambridge University, at a very prestigious paediatric conference. This conference was only open to consultants and other senior doctors. Grandad was allowed to go – but not as a consultant paediatrician but as my guest. On another occasion Grandad had been involved in a case where a maverick doctor had suggested children had not been injured by their parents, but were suffering from ‘temporary brittle bone disease’, a disease which he had invented. Grandad was very upset about how the doctor and his lawyer had tried to manipulate the court proceedings and wrote to the President of the Royal College of Paediatrics saying the doctor should be stopped and the College needed to do something. Nothing happened with all the information that Grandad had sent in, but some time later I got a request, from the editor of a law journal, who said that she had been contacted by the Royal College and would I write an article about the doctor.

While I was working there was a very important Act which changed the law – The Children Act 1989. A new system was introduced whereby people who were dissatisfied with how they had been treated by Social Services could complain. Under the Act independent people had to be appointed to investigate complaints and sit on complaints panels. I thought that would be an interesting thing to do, and as I was working half time had the time to do it. So I applied to be an independent person under this scheme. I was appointed for Nottinghamshire and sat on the first complaints panel in the county. I also did some very interesting investigations. After I retired I carried on working for Nottinghamshire and Nottingham City and I still do this to this day, although now I only sit on panels and there are less and less of these.

I had one big success as an academic. Mary was also a family lawyer and she and I collaborated to write a book. We entered it for a competition, set up by the biggest law publishers. We were short-listed for the final, along with 4 other books. Sadly we did not win. However, after only one edition the winning book was not brought out again, but our book, which is now written by 2 other people, is still going strong. Also, I was told by a friend of one of the judges that there was a big argument about whether or not we should be the winners. I have no idea if that is true or not, but I like to think it is.

For a bit of non-academic fun with my students, every year when Comic Relief was running I would do something for it and get my students to sponsor me. One year I decided to be very brave. As the last 'official' night of Comic Relief is always a Friday, I invited them to sponsor me to wear my red dressing gown at work all day, which I knew would include walking across the university campus in it in order to get to my lecture. I felt an absolute idiot, but I did it and raised money, which of course was the idea. However, my favourite bit of fun, which I did several times, was to ask students to enter my competition. This competition had the question: what did Grandad give me for Christmas one year? The students had to guess the answer. No-one ever got the answer correct, although one year a student came very close by guessing a toilet brush. The actual answer was - a luxury wooden toilet seat!

Snapshots of life when your mums were growing up

You can all ask your mums about their lives as they were growing up, but this is a little bit of how I remember it.

Life at home was great fun. The four girls played a lot together and if one of them had fallen out with another one it didn't matter, they had always got another sister to play with. Their particular favourites were playing with Care Bears and My Little Ponies, in the summer going on the slippy slide, and sliding down the stairs on mattresses. We used to like having children round, so there were often lots of children in the house. Katie, Richard and Alison from number 30 Highland Grove were round regularly, as was Joanna Richardson, who lived at number 14.

Another favourite activity was to put on a show. Claire always organised the shows and she had the main role, or was narrator. Anna would be given the next most important part, Sarah a part but usually a smaller one, and Rachel would be the crowd. The best show was the one they did to a tape about Moses. Sadly I don't what happened to that tape, as it made for an excellent show.

On Sunday we would nearly always go swimming. That took some organising, as what would happen is that I would put a joint in the oven, with potatoes, and prepare the rest of the vegetables. We would then go swimming, with Grandad taking usually Sarah and Rachel in to the men's changing rooms, until they were too old to go in them. Then we would come home to a roast dinner. Surprisingly I can only recall one time, although there may have been more, when Grandad got called in to the hospital whilst we were at swimming.

At the time Rachel was born Grandad got a second consultant colleague, Jane Bodden, who came to work with him. However, that still meant he was on call every other day. Because Grandad was on call so much it meant he was quite often late home or knew he was likely to be called in. This meant if one child needed to go out e.g. to brownies, all of them had to go. So particularly in winter I had to dress them all up, go to brownies, bring them back home, then dress them up again to go out to pick up from brownies.

All your mums learned to play at least one musical instrument and all achieved a good standard. All of them took music GCSE and all got As for their exam. Claire also got an A at A level for music. Both Claire and Sarah were chosen for free violin lessons through the peripatetic music system. Anna wanted to play the recorder at first and then she took up the flute as well. Rachel chose to play the cello. She told me when she was older that the reason she had chosen the cello was because she heard me saying one day that my favourite instrument was the cello. As we had a piano in the house they also played the piano, with all of them going for piano lessons. We had the general rule that music practice took place first thing in the morning, so that practice would not be something they had hanging over them in the evening after a hard day at school and homework.

Just before Rachel was born we bought a new car, as we needed one that would take four children. At that time people carriers were an entirely new idea and when we bought our Toyota Spacecruiser people used to come up and peer in the windows and stop me and ask about it, because it was so unusual. We had that car for 19 years, so it served us well. Going on holiday we always went by car. At first we stayed in England. One year, when Rachel was 2, we stayed at Butlins in Skegness. As we went from our holiday chalet to the play area a man on guard duty greeted us and said 'Hello duck' to Rachel. She very indignantly replied 'I'm not a duck. I'm Wachel', (at the time she couldn't say her Rs).

The year Rachel was 3 we thought she was now old enough to cope with the journey, so we started going to France for our holidays. I am sure your mums will have lots of stories about those holidays. We used to stay in little villages, usually near the sea, and we had lots of bread, cheese and pate meals, which Grandad and I loved. One year we went with the Bettle family and stayed in a chateau outside Paris. The Bettles had brought a skateboard on holiday with them and all the children used to have a lovely time racing round the corridors of the chateau on the skateboard. On one very hot day we visited Paris and while we were waiting to get into the Louvre, because it was so hot and there was a large pond with a fountain outside, we let the children jump about in the water. At first no other children joined in, but after a while lots of other children joined them. Back at the chateau all the children got together and put on a very good version of Matilda, with Sarah, somewhat surprisingly, having the leading role of Matilda. Anna was Miss Honey and Claire Miss Trunchbull. Rachel, as usual, was just one of the children in the class.

Whilst we were still living at the top of the road, on days that I was working I would pile Claire, Anna and Sarah into the car and pick up Katie and Richard as well, to take them to school. At that time Rachel and Alison were too little to go to school. Some mornings Traude, who lived next door to the Terrys and was very eccentric, would come out and whilst I was in a hurry to get the children to school and then drive off to work, she would insist on washing all the windows of the car. Traude also came round to our garden one day and insisted on planting Jerusalem artichokes in the garden, even though we did not want them. I can also remember going round to her house one time and being fed a pie which was made using the peeled skins of fruit. Yuk.

Some snippets about your mums

Once we had come back from Canada and before we moved to Worksop, we lived in our old house in Sheffield for a few months. During that time when I was at work Claire went to a nursery school and Anna to a childminder. One day when I went to pick up Claire the teacher told me that at story time a little boy, called Monim, would not sit down, so the teacher had had to tell Monim more than once to sit down. After she had done so Claire piped up saying 'Sit down Monim, sit down Monim' and didn't stop, until Claire, too, was causing havoc in the class.

Claire was quite forward at reading and writing so when she started school, aged 5 (as in those days you started school as close to your 5th birthday as possible, starting either at the beginning of the term, or immediately after half term), she was already ahead of many of the children who had been at school since the previous September. Claire had a particular friend, Amy Coxhill, and Amy's mother, Linda, told me that at parents evening Claire and Amy's teacher had spent time telling Linda what a genius Claire was. It is a good job Linda and I were good friends, as it is not very tactful to tell a parent how clever another child than their own is.

When Claire was 7 she started having piano lessons and about 6 weeks after she started her piano teacher had a concert in which all of her pupils played. She arranged for a friend of hers, Benjamin Frith, who is (and was then) a well-known piano soloist throughout the world, to come along and to give a prize to the best player in each half of the concert, the younger ones being in the first half. To my great surprise and delight he chose Claire. I felt very proud. Not long after this Claire and I were at the Worksop music festival and we saw Benjamin Frith. I said to Claire 'Do you know who that is?' Claire took a long, hard look at him and then said 'Is it Mozart?'

Of course I was proud of all your Mums as they were growing up, so as I have mentioned one incident where Claire was involved I will tell you of a time which involved each of them, though of course there were loads more. So, picking some of my favourites and Anna first. When Anna was in Brownies there was a photo competition in Nottinghamshire for Brownies and Guides and a photo by Anna was chosen as one of the winning entries and put on display. Moving on to Sarah, when she was in class 4 at primary school she (and another girl, they shared it) was chosen for the lead role in the school production of Snow White. The 7 dwarves were all in year 6 and all were taller than Sarah. Lastly Rachel. When she was in year 7 at secondary school, at the Christmas service they had a string quartet to play to the audience. Claire and 2 other girls were in year 13 and all three were doing music A level. They played the two violin parts and the viola and Rachel played the cello.

A funny story about Rachel being in year 7 and Claire in year 13 was when both were involved in a school play. Claire always used to get roped in to playing the violin in the orchestra by the music teacher. A boy in the year above Rachel, called Christian, who was taking part in the play, saw Claire and said very importantly "I know that girl". Rachel responded by saying well she also knew Claire. Christian then said "I bet I know her better than you do". You can imagine Rachel's enjoyment at responding to that one.

When I was growing up some of my favourite books were ones about Milly Molly Mandy. Amongst the stories my absolute favourite was one where Milly Molly Mandy has an attic room transformed into a bedroom for her. This gave me the idea to do something a bit like that for Claire and Anna, who shared a bedroom in the attic. Whilst we were away on holiday I arranged for a decorator to come in and decorate the bedroom with Care Bear wallpaper. I had also bought some Care Bear pillow cases and duvet covers and asked Rebel to put them on the beds. So, when we got back from holiday I sent the two of them upstairs, pretending I wanted them to get something from their room, and watched very excitedly as they discovered their transformed room. I think I was as pleased as they were about the room.

Anna was nearly always the most placid, good and easy going of the 4 girls. However, when she was very little she liked being in the dark in the house and if I tried to take her outside into the garden she would cry. Things also seemed to happen to her. One day I got a call from school to say that she had been walking past an open window at school when the hinge broke and the window had fallen on her head. She also managed to break her wrist one day, when she was roller-skating. One day, when she was quite little, I asked her what she wanted to be when she grew up and she replied she wanted to be a fairy and work at the university.

Talking of Anna being good, of course she was not always good, in the same way that Sarah, who was usually the one who got up to mischief, was not always the one who had done something naughty. This was evident one day when I went to the piano and found that someone had been scribbling on the piano keys. I immediately suspected Sarah and called her down and showed them to her. She protested that she hadn't done it, but I did not really believe her, as it was just the sort of thing I would have expected her to do. However, I was being very unfair, as Anna then came to me and said that it wasn't Sarah who had done this, it was her.

Anna was not the only one who broke a limb when she was little, Sarah twice broke something. Once she broke right at the top of her arm and on another occasion she broke her wrist, falling off a bouncy castle. The time she broke her arm she was very unlucky. By this time the Terry Family had moved away from Worksop to Norfolk and had invited Sarah and Anna to go and stay with them. One day Janet rang me up to tell me that Sarah had fallen out of a tree, but that she was ok. Janet said she had taken Sarah to the doctor's who had told her that nothing was broken, and to try and exercise Sarah's arm. I had arranged to pick Sarah and Anna up about half way between our two houses and as I stood waiting to get them I could see Janet walking along the road, holding Sarah's hand and trying to swing her arm. Being her mum I could see immediately that she had broken it. So as soon as we got back to Worksop I took her up to the hospital, where sure enough they could see the break on an x-ray. Poor Janet was quite upset that she had been doing completely the wrong thing with Sarah, though it wasn't actually Janet's fault. It was bad enough breaking her arm, but then another blow. For a few years we used to go down to Seaford to stay in a house near Grandad's sister, Mary, and Joe and Joanna. Shortly after Sarah had broken her arm we went there as usual. One day we took all the children into Brighton and went to the funfair on the pier. All the children wanted to go on the ghost train, but because it was a bumpy ride we had to say that Sarah could not go, because as the break was so high up it was not possible to put her arm in a pot and she could therefore damage her arm. So, all the others had a lovely time on the ghost train and all she could do was stand and wait. No wonder she was upset.

When Rachel was little she was the wimpiest child alive, I think. She was very, very shy and got upset any time she was left with anyone or any time someone came to visit. One time my nephew Richard came to visit out of the blue. I was really pleased to see him and was looking forward to a lovely conversation with him. However, Rachel would not stop crying because he was in the house, and in the end he just had to leave. In fact Rachel remained largely a wimp until, very oddly, the day of Allan's funeral. Audrey and Allan had moved up to Worksop when Rachel was about 2, as Allan had been very ill and they wanted to be near someone in the family. So, when Allan died, the funeral was in Worksop and after it everyone came back to our house. Rachel, instead of being completely overwhelmed, as she would usually have been, suddenly transformed and spent most of the time leaping off the settee and generally showing off to everyone, making them laugh and cheering everyone up.

Rachel did not completely reform overnight, and when she first started school she used to cry every day when I left her. Her teacher, Miss Saynor, would take her onto her knee to comfort her and one day she told her teacher, who was young and pretty, 'My daddy says that he would like to sit on your knee'.

As the girls got older we started having boyfriends coming round to the house and the girls would disappear off for the evening to go to pubs and parties. I never liked them going out and coming back late in the evening, but obviously they had to be allowed to go. What particularly impressed me about all your mums was that they would tell me when they would be back, and they would be back by the time they said.

I was really sad when Claire went off to university, the first child to leave home, as I knew this was just the beginning and in time all of them would go. I am not sure that it got any easier as each child left. I loved having my girls at home and simply wanted it to continue, though I knew it couldn't.

We now come to the worst event of all, the death of John, who lived next door. Phil and Jane had moved in next door when John was a baby. Then George came along when John was a little over 2, and Phil and Jane looked upon their family as complete. The boys were lovely little boys and used to spend a lot of time round at our house. Until we put a gate in the fence, they used to like climbing over the fence to come into our garden. Your mums used to baby sit them and Anna went away on holiday with the Browns to help look after them. John was 8 when he died from a bleed on the brain whilst staying with his grandparents in Sookholme. John meant a lot to me and Grandad, and it was dreadful. I shan't say any more than that.

My medical escapade

In Grandad's memoirs you will have heard a lot about medical matters. I have no medical stories to tell, apart from one involving me. In 2005 Rachel was back living at home temporarily and working in Sheffield. One of my colleagues at work persuaded me and Grandad to be part of a charity quiz team, the quiz happening in the evening. Grandad was going to work in Doncaster that day, so Rachel said she would give me a lift to Sheffield, then we wouldn't have 2 cars in Sheffield in the evening. As she had to get to work earlier than me, Rachel drove to where she worked and dropped me off. I then had about a 30 minute walk to get to work. I started walking to work and can remember being aware that the buildings around me were flashing. The next thing I knew I woke up in a hospital bed. Very soon after I woke up Grandad walked in to where I was lying and said to me: 'Do you know who I am?' which I thought was a ridiculous question and replied yes, of course I did.

There was a good medical reason for the question from Grandad, who had an absolutely horrible time until I said that to him. He was at work in Doncaster and got a phone call from his secretary to say to go straight to Sheffield, as I had been in an accident. Of course Grandad knew that I set off in a car with Rachel, so he tried to ring Rachel. But Rachel was at work and not allowed to answer her phone on private calls, so didn't answer. So poor Grandad was not only worrying about me, but about Rachel, as well, wondering if we had been in a road accident and what had happened to both of us. Fortunately he kept trying Rachel, who after a while realised that Grandad was desperately trying to get hold of her, so went to the loo to answer her phone. That put Grandad's mind at rest about her, but not me. The information he had been given included the fact that I had blood coming out of my ears. This can be a sign of a serious head injury with brain damage. That is why he asked me if I knew who he was.

What had happened to me was that I had collapsed in the street and on falling hit my jaw. This fractured my jaw in 3 places, including fracturing one of the hinges of my jaw, which has unfortunately never mended properly, and I still cannot move my jaw normally. It was this that was causing the blood to come out of my ear. I was in hospital for about 4 days and was then allowed home. Because I had broken my jaw I could not open my mouth very much and mumbled as I talked. Also, I could only eat very soft food for a while. Once I was a bit better I wrote to the ambulance service to ask them to tell me what had happened. I cannot remember any of the next bit of the story but this is what they told me. Passers by had found me and apparently I was trying to get up off the floor, but couldn't. When the ambulance arrived the crew tried to put a collar on my neck, in case I had damaged my spine, but I just took it off, and when they asked me my name I would not tell them. My ambulance report states that 'the patient was uncooperative'! A bit of drama I also missed was that the ambulance blue lit me to hospital.

Because of what had happened to me I had to go and see a neurologist, who asked me to describe what I remembered. When I said about the buildings flashing his next question to me was 'Have you had an epileptic fit before?' Both Grandad and I obviously did not want it to be epilepsy, but as he diagnosed epilepsy I had to give up my driving licence for a year. The neurologist said that after one fit 70% of people went on to have another and unfortunately he proved to be right. About 9 months later I was in a shop in Worksop and things started flashing. Grandad had warned me to get down on the floor if that happened which I did, so I did not hurt myself, but I did manage to knock down a pile of boxes of popcorn on top of myself. Once again, the next thing I knew was waking up in hospital.

Grandad, of course, got called in to the hospital, but this time he wasn't worried, he was annoyed. The reason he was annoyed was because he wasn't told why he was being called in. He was not on call and he thought he was being called when he shouldn't be. This was another evening when we were not going to be just staying at home as normal. Jane next door was away, so Phil had invited us to join him for a meal of fish and chips. Not surprisingly, Phil, too, started getting annoyed, as he had bought the fish and chips and we were nowhere to be found. Somewhat late, after seeing me in hospital, Grandad went round next door to explain what had happened. Grandad wanted to know exactly what had happened in the shop, so he took the fish and chips that Phil had bought and went up the road and through the hospital grounds, eating them on the way, to get to the shop. As he was leaving the hospital grounds he wrapped the fish and chips up and popped them in a rubbish bin. He then went to the shop and when the shop assistant told him what had occurred he realised, from the description, that I had definitely had an epileptic fit. He then left to come back to see me in hospital. On the way back he stopped to pick up his fish and chips out of the bin. As he did so a porter who worked at the hospital saw him taking them out - and start eating them. Needless to say the story about Grandad eating food out of a rubbish bin quickly spread around the hospital.

Because I had had another fit I had to give up my driving licence for another year, which in a funny sort of way was a good thing. I had read that when people give up their licences they promise that once they get it back they will not go back to their previous ways and will not use their car, but they nearly always do. I thought about that and decided that I definitely would not go back to using the car. I would carry on using public transport to get to work and would carry on walking to do all my shopping. I am glad to say I stuck to my resolution and I still only use the car when I have to. I do all my shopping, including heavy supermarket shopping using a trolley, and I use public transport whenever I can.

The sons in law

Grandad and I count ourselves hugely lucky for having the best sons in law in the world, just like we have the best daughters in the world. I had nothing to do with Sarah meeting James, or

Rachel meeting David, but I did play an important part in Claire and Matthew meeting.

Claire rang me up shortly before my birthday in August 2007 and said she would come and visit on my birthday. As Claire has always been a bit hopeless about remembering things like birthdays, it may have been a guilty conscience which made her decide to visit. Also, the previous Christmas she had given Grandad 2 Christmas presents and me none. I am sure she meant to give me a present, but she was just being her usual hopeless self. We decided that it would be nice to go out for a meal, and we went to a Chinese restaurant in Worksop. Whilst we were eating I got a text message on my phone from Anna saying that she and Sarah had gone speed dating in Leeds. They had met a chap there, who they did not think was suitable for either of them, but who they thought would suit Claire, and that I knew him from work. This, of course, was Matthew.

I thought about this a bit and realised that they would get on well together, so I told Claire about the message I had received. Claire asked me some questions about Matthew and a fairly key thing I said to her was that he reminded me of her cousin, Peter, the one who visited us in Canada. Claire has always liked Peter a lot, so was interested in what I had to say. The next day I got a message from Anna, telling me that Claire had been asking her about Matthew. I thought it would be a good idea if they met so the next day at work I summonsed Matthew to my office. When he came to see me I said that I had heard about his visit to Leeds, and that if he was prepared to go speed dating he should be prepared to go on a blind date. I then gave him Claire's contact details. As I was very senior at work and Matthew was just starting out on his career he may well have felt he had to contact Claire. Anyway, the rest, as they say, is history and one year later, on my birthday, Claire and Matthew got married.

When Grandad and I met James and Matthew we knew instantly how well Sarah and Rachel had chosen and were thrilled when they decided to get married. The three weddings have been three of the best days in our lives and we have been proved right to be thrilled. However, not only have we gained the best three sons in law, we have also gained sort of sons in law in Etienne and Paul, who we were delighted to include in our family. And now, of course, we have the very best 9 grandchildren in the world. How lucky can you get?

Retirement

Grandad and I had planned that we would retire together in the summer when I turned 60, as that was when I became entitled to both my state pension and my university pension. However, I had the most tremendous stroke of luck. The year before I was due to go the university needed to save money, so it set up a scheme to encourage people to leave. Basically the scheme was that if you went you would get one year's pay plus your pension would be as if you had stayed on for the year. For me that was the perfect offer. I could go a year earlier than I intended, but still get paid for that year and get the same pension, so I snapped up the offer. I even got 2 extra months of pay out of it, as the year ran from October and I was due to leave at the end of August.

In the run up to leaving at the end of October I was a bit concerned as I did not know what I was going to do with my time. I had not planned anything. However, I then had another stroke of luck. At the beginning of November a newly formed Worksop U3A met for the first time. I read about it in the local paper and went to the first meeting. At the meeting all sorts of groups were set up and people were invited to join in any they fancied. I joined the walking group and the reading group, two of my favourite activities, at that meeting and have been a member of them ever since. Since then I have joined musical groups, steel band, recorder and ukulele, as well. I got a bit bored with ukulele, so have given that up, but I still love playing the recorder and go to that in both Worksop and Retford, and I go to steel band and run the practices.

Through the U3A I have met a lot of people and now count a number of people as friends. When I was working I did not really socialise in Worksop, my friends were all from Sheffield, so it is nice now to have some friends who live close by. One particular friend I have made is Jenny, who I met through steel band. Her husband, John, is a chemist by training and he and Grandad get on very well together. So we have all been on holiday together on a number of occasions and it has been very successful.

I haven't talked much about holidays, other than to tell you a bit about the ones in France with your mums. We do like going away and have had some lovely times largely in Europe, usually with members of my family. We regularly go away with Janet and the rest of her family, and have also been with my other two sisters. We've also gone on holiday with Grandad's sister Mary, although that has not always worked out perfectly. We arranged to go to Ireland with them one year, Grandad doing all the arranging. As we were flying in to different airports in Belfast we arranged that Grandad and I would meet Mary and Joe at their airport, as were arriving first. So we got a taxi over to the airport and waited for them to arrive. However, when everyone got off the plane there was no Mary and Joe. We hung around for ages and waited for another flight from England, but still no-one. Eventually Grandad rang Joe and asked where they were. In England, Joe said puzzled. Somehow dates had got muddled, so we went one week and Joe and Mary went a week later.

On Grandad's 65th birthday we went on our longest trip, as we flew to New Zealand, where Stephen lives. Two of his daughters were getting married, a fortnight apart, so we decided to go over for the weddings and travel around for the days in between. We had a brilliant time over there, but I absolutely hated the travel, so I don't think we will ever go back.

So I am now getting to the end of this story. The pandemic has put an end to planned holidays for this year so far, although luckily just before lockdown we had a trip to Morocco for 2 weeks with Janet. We have missed a holiday in Majorca, with Janet and family, booked for Easter and, even worse, we won't be going to Reighton this year for the annual weekend with all you grandchildren and your parents. However, we are hoping to arrange something nice over the summer, so you won't miss out altogether.

I have kept myself very busy during the pandemic, doing my bit to help. Early on my sister Alison mentioned that she was sewing scrubs bags for NHS workers. When she said that I knew that that was something I could do, so for many weeks all I ever seemed to do was to cut out and sew scrubs bags. I estimate that I made about 450 bags. Fortunately, they now have enough, and I don't have to make any more. I have also done more sewing, making dresses and tops for you girls and shirts for the boys, using material I was given. I enjoyed doing that. I am a bit bored by not being allowed to go to any U3A activities, not being allowed until recently to meet friends or family, and even now still being restricted in what I can do. However, I also think I am very lucky. I have Grandad to keep me company. We live in a lovely big house which I can enjoy and have a beautiful garden, looked after by Grandad. I have seen all of you grandchildren, which is by far the most important thing, so I don't really have anything to complain about.

All in all I count myself an incredibly lucky person, who has had a great life. I had a happy childhood and as an adult I did a job I enjoyed. Most important of all, I met Grandad. We suit each other and have been very happy together. What I hope for all 9 of you is that you have just as lovely life as I have had. If that happens, the world is a wonderful place.

I want to finish by saying: I LOVE YOU ALL.

Lots and lots of love, Granny

Leonard Hugh Paul Williams – A Celebration

Monday 16th January 2023

Good afternoon everyone.

My name is Matthew, and I am one of Leonard's sons-in-law. I have been asked by Catherine and Leonard's four daughters first and foremost to thank so many of you for coming out this afternoon to celebrate Leonard's life with us. It's truly humbling to see such a turnout here for Leonard.

I have also been asked to say a few words about Len. It's a true privilege to do so, if a bit of a daunting one. I was equally privileged some years ago, at my wedding in fact, to enjoy a speech made by Leonard himself which was in part about me. On that occasion Leonard said – and I think I'm quoting him correctly here – "Matthew has come along and, well, he is really, really, weird".

I'm pretty confident that this was a good thing in Leonard's eyes and all I can say is that I hope this weird son-in-law will be able to do some justice to a marvelous and loving but – yes – definitely also very weird father-in-law.

It's clear from the numbers here today, and the more I know are watching us stream this, how many people's lives were touched by Leonard Hugh Paul Williams. To his family he was of course a loving husband, father, grandfather, brother to Vincent and Mary, and uncle. To others here he was a neighbour. To many, of course, he was a doctor. And to a few, he was an allotment enthusiast who managed to grow asparagus and artichokes in Worksop despite being repeatedly told it was impossible.

Sorry, I just know Leonard would want me to get that point in here somewhere.

However, we all knew Leonard, and whether we had the privilege to know him well or more fleetingly, all that knew him knew him to be uniquely generous. Generous with his time and generous with his advice. He helped and counselled people when they needed it, he gave people comfort and consolation when they needed it. During the recent COVID lockdowns Leonard decided to sit down and write his autobiography, and I'll refer to it a few times here. At one point he simply says "I like being asked to do things for others". This of course was never truer than when Leonard was engaged in what became his life calling of practicing medicine, and specifically when he was taking care of sick children, babies, and frequently – in his own special way – their parents.

It is only right to reflect on Leonard's remarkable achievements as a doctor, which I'm sure is how a lot of people here will have known him. He of course came to work at Bassetlaw Hospital as a consultant pediatrician in 1980, where he stayed for thirty years until his retirement in 2010. But before then, as a student and then whilst working his way up from being a junior doctor, he had already practised medicine or been involved in medical research in some six or seven countries and five continents. These included Ethiopia, where he waded in the rivers of the Dire Dawa region dodging pythons and crocodiles to collect snails for testing. He also paid the locals in cigarettes in return for samples of their poo and wee.

Those locals by the way – so Leonard once told me – were quite bemused by all this and quickly reached the not-unreasonable conclusion that this enthusiastic and friendly foreigner who had suddenly descended into their midst was utterly insane.

Leonard next worked in India, seeing lots of patients with tropical diseases, typhoid, leprosy, and malaria. He spent time in New Guinea where he worked with patients from an Eastern Highlands tribe who were allegedly cannibals. They were suffering from an unidentified disease which later turned out to be CJD, the human form of mad cow disease. Leonard deduced that the disease was spreading within the tribe through their practice of ritualistically eating parts of their dead relatives. After qualifying Leonard also spent some time treating children and adults in Zambia, where he was amongst the first doctors in the world to observe a mysterious, unidentified syndrome. Some mistook it for sleeping sickness but, as it transpired, it was in fact the beginnings of the AIDS pandemic.

Of course, Leonard also spent two years living and working in Canada, where his second daughter, Anna, was born, before eventually coming back to work in Bassetlaw. Once there he would transform the paediatric department, championing modernizations that would make it one of the most respected in the country. His medical contributions and influence were felt throughout the region and, in the words of his former NHS trust "Health services in North Nottinghamshire are better today as a result of his guidance".

All of this sounds rather grand and fantastical I know, and I think Leonard would rather approve of that, being a man not above the occasional embellishment of a good story. There's a paragraph near the end of his autobiography that I like where he writes "I do tell lies from time to time but never to gain advantage or to hurt someone; they are just for fun. For instance, do you believe that I really and truly did go to India when I was a student, or is that just a lie?"

I checked by the way, and he did indeed go to India. He did not however play tennis with John McEnroe. Nor was there a diamond worth millions of pounds randomly protruding from a wall in his garden at Highland Grove, which his daughters were sworn to guard and protect with their very lives.

Of course, fun embellishments aside, Leonard was actually unflinchingly honest in most things. He would particularly love to tell the story of how he was at school the morning after the death of King George VI. He'd been spotted crying in assembly by the headteacher (who also happened to be his grandma). Leonard was brought out to the front and a proud grandma stoically asked him to explain to the whole school why he was so sad on this most significant day of national tragedy. Leonard proceeded to explain in front of the assembled children how his budgie, Joey, had also died during the night and how devastated he was about this.

Leonard lived and breathed medicine, as almost anyone here can attest. He was born in 1945 in Castlewellan in Northern Ireland and had grown up hearing the story of how his grandfather, Dote, had operated on a young catholic agitator, Jimmy Johnson, who had been shot in the chest during the troubles. Dote had had Jimmy brought into his house, when no other local doctor would help. The same house where Leonard would later be born. Dote had then removed the bullet with Jimmy lying on the pantry table. Dote would be ostracized from the local - predominantly protestant - community for doing this. Dote had also taught Leonard a great deal about nature and birds specifically, which were interests Leonard nurtured for the rest of his life.

When it comes to his medical work in Worksop, however, there is no greater testament to Leonard's career here than the reaction he would so often receive from people in the local community when they spotted him out and about. Walking with Leonard through Worksop, before and after he retired, was honestly sometimes akin to being with an A-list celebrity, albeit one who had a penchant for flat caps and dried fruit. People would come up to him and ask "are you Dr. Williams?" and when he indicated he was the person would frequently get emotional and recall the story of how Leonard had treated their child years ago, or saved their own life as an infant. Leonard would always listen carefully and in most cases would remember the case in clear detail and ask the person how they or their family were getting on. Leonard himself, it must be said, never sought out any such attention, in his autobiography he wrote of these occasions "I am pleased after ex-patients come up to me to say how good I had been to them but I find it uncomfortable and embarrassing at the time".

Of course, all these former patients and their families felt, I'm absolutely certain, was a genuine and heartfelt affection for the man they knew had helped them through one of the most difficult periods of their lives. To these people Leonard wasn't a globe-trotting scientist, even one who traded wee and poo for cigarettes. He wasn't even a great modernizer or innovator in the field of paediatrics. Most often, to these people Leonard Williams was simply the doctor who would get up in the middle of the night, leave his house in his pyjamas and dressing gown, walk the short distance down the road to the hospital and then, still in his pyjamas and dressing gown, check in on the sick children and the premature babies to make sure they were ok.

When Leonard's passing was announced recently on Facebook it was met with over 400 comments from people sharing the most heartfelt memories of him, many recalling how he'd helped them or their children when they were young. I can tell you Leonard's family have read every single one of these comments and collectively they make a truly beautiful tribute to a wonderful father and husband, and a huge thank you goes from the family to everyone who contributed to that.

It is to Leonard's role as a family man that I now want to turn attention. For as much as Leonard's life was committed to medicine, he was first and foremost a dedicated family man who took the most pleasure in life out of being a husband to Catherine, a father to his four daughters and later a grandfather to nine beautiful youngsters. Writing his autobiography at the height of the COVID lockdowns Leonard wrote of himself and of Catherine, "The thing we miss most at this time is our four daughters and their families". Of his grandchildren he wrote "I am particularly fascinated by the grandchildren. I am enormously impressed by their huge range of diverse talents and I am proud of the way that their parents work to facilitate and encourage these developments".

Now this of course all started when Leonard met Catherine in 1977. It was at a dinner arranged primarily as a meetup between herself, Leonard and Catherine's cousin Peter Todd, who Leonard had previously met and worked with in Zambia. It's clear from Leonard's autobiography that he was smitten straight away with Catherine. He describes the young Catherine Todd as "a good-looking lady without the need for glamour paraphernalia". Leonard needed a plan, and so he fell back on his tried and tested strategy which I alluded to a little earlier. He…told a porky. On the spot he concocted a housewarming party he said he was in the process of arranging, and he asked Catherine if she would like to come. She agreed, leaving Leonard in a small quandary given that no such party had been even at the planning stages in his mind ten seconds earlier.

The party did happen eventually, although only after Catherine had rung Leonard to 'remind' him about it. They spent time together the following weekend that and, well, to cut a long story short, as Leonard wrote in his autobiography "We have rarely been separated from each other for the whole day in the 43 years since then".

Much more recently, when Leonard was still in hospital and in isolation, Catherine heard a poem on the radio which she sent in to be read to Leonard by the nurses. She said in a note to Leonard that "I knew immediately it was perfect, just how I feel about you". The poem is by Edwin Muir and I thought I'd take a moment now to read it before I go on talking a little more about Leonard.

The Confirmation
by Edwin Muir

Yes, yours, my love, is the right human face.
I in my mind had waited for this long,
Seeing the false and searching for the true,
Then found you as a traveler finds a place
Of welcome suddenly amid the wrong
Valleys and rocks and twisting roads. But you,
What shall I call you? A fountain in a waste,
A well of water in a country dry,
Or anything that's honest and good, an eye
That makes the whole world bright. Your open heart,
Simple with giving, gives the primal deed,
The first good world, the blossom, the blowing seed,
The hearth, the steadfast land, the wandering sea,
Not beautiful or rare in every part,
But like yourself, as they were meant to be.

In those 40-plus years between Catherine and Leonard meeting and getting married the Williams family grew and expanded and had more wonderful memories than I can possibly get across here. Of course, some of those memories may have seemed less wonderful at the time. If you ask Catherine or any of Leonard's children they can tell you in much greater detail than I can about the time the family were on a holiday in France and their car broke down on the motorway. Now, one of the things I haven't said yet about Len is that he loved to study foreign languages. In fact, those that visited them at Highland Grove might remember seeing whole bookcases and shelves stuffed full with foreign-language dictionaries of French, German, Italian, Spanish etc…

Catherine and Leonard both would later mount a long term but ultimately futile campaign of trying to parcel off the many dictionaries to their various daughters, claiming they would be extremely useful to the grandchildren.

…Anyway, so being in France and being broken down in the years before mobile phones, Leonard took it upon himself to go to the roadside emergency phone to convey to the operator on the other end their predicament and to ask for help to be sent. Leonard dutifully did so in his very best French.

Not long later, in fact surprisingly not long later, and apparently moving at great speed along the hard shoulder, the emergency services arrived in the form not of a tow truck or mechanic, but several police cars flashing their lights, along with an ambulance. As the police arrived, they jumped out of their cars and did not so much ask Leonard if he needed help as confront him loudly and somewhat aggressively with several quite surprising questions about what he was doing there. After some initial confusion you see, it had transpired that instead of communicating to the operator something like "Our car has broken down on the motorway and we

are in need of roadside assistance" what Leonard had actually said, somehow, was "Come quickly, I have murdered my father".

Once again, Leonard could be prone to exaggeration...even without actually trying.

Much as Leonard loved foreign languages, it has to be said he seems to have sometimes been unable to master his own. By his own gleeful admission his spelling was utterly atrocious. He writes in his autobiography "I was, and still am, hopeless at spelling and very slow at reading". There is one story I'll tell you in which Leonard was trying to pay with a cheque at the supermarket. The cheque was for forty-five pounds. Leonard wrote it out and gave it to the shop assistant at the till who regarded it, looked up at Leonard and informed him that she couldn't accept the cheque because she didn't believe the cheque book was his. You see, she had seen that the cheques belonged to one Dr. Leonard HP Williams. But she had also seen that the man before her had managed to misspell both the word 'forty' and the word 'five' on his cheque. Fortunately, a kind individual further back in the queue who knew Leonard vouched for him and he was able to leave that day with this shopping.

So, whilst Leonard may not have murdered anyone on the side of a motorway that day in France, he could unquestionably murder the odd verb or noun. This is something I can attest to myself, I mean, I've read his autobiography. At one point there he talks about working in a baby unit in the hospital, and he spells unit "y-o-u-n-i-t". Then in the next sentence he points out to the reader "I've just noticed how I've made the best of my many spelling mistakes"

You know, I'm personally certain Leonard occasionally did these things on purpose. He says in his autobiography, when he's talking about his time at Cambridge University, "People say it's for posh people. Well, nobody has ever said I am posh". Leonard was definitely not posh. In fact I know to the members of Catherine's steel band group, Leonard will forever be associated with drains, after he told them once how for years he had annually rodded the house drains at Highland Grove on the night of the vernal equinox.

Leonard was absolutely self-effacing about most things, certainly with his family. He was not the sort to complain, even though he suffered dreadfully living for over 40 years with a wife who is pathologically against turning the central heating on. Picture, if you will, the sight seared into my memory of Catherine lying on her side of the bed in a bedroom which, at her insistence, has no modern double-glazing. Catherine is throwing off the bedclothes and proclaiming “It's like an oven in here!”. Meanwhile, on his side of the bed Leonard has cocooned himself under three extra blankets. He is wearing gloves and a woolly hat, in bed. He rubs his fingers together in a vain attempt to keep his circulation going.

Of course, I know the real question you all have now is – what am I doing there?

I'm coming to the end now. As I've hopefully managed to share with you this afternoon, Leonard was first and foremost a warm and loving family man (although obviously often not warm in the literal sense as I have just explained). I do remember about a year ago when Leonard was in hospital after his accident, we were speaking to him on video-link and he called me over. I later found out he'd done the same thing with his other sons-in law, David and James. He told me he loved me and that he thought I was an excellent son-in-law. And that was lovely. He then said we should discuss this more, and that in fact we should set aside an hour the next day so he could talk more to me about how he loved me.

Of course, being a very stereotypical British man, reserved and possibly emotionally stilted, I thought “AN HOUR?!” Fortunately, by the next day he'd forgotten and I breathed a great sigh of relief.

Leonard didn't need an hour to explain how he loved his family and others that were close to him. He had made that obvious by his complete devotion to those he cared about for the forty years before. He put others first, always, whether that was in his medical career or in his own home life. He was a man utterly committed to his family and took the most pleasure in life from seeing them grow, develop, and succeed around him whilst he often remained unassumingly in the background, maybe slipping on an extra layer against the cold.

In the last chapter of Leonard's autobiography, my father-in-law becomes a little reflective. The chapter is titled "Am I normal?" In the chapter he reflects on aspects of himself and his personality, and especially on those things he thinks people might see as unusual about him. So, he talks about the fact he doesn't really care for going out to pubs or parties. He notes that most of his clothes are second hand…

He actually gave me quite a few clothes over the years, which I love to wear. My wife's therapy bill isn't really that costly at all.

…Leonard also reflects on the fact he can't spell, that he doesn't like spending money on himself and that, as I've said, just occasionally, he will tell lies.

At the end of his autobiography Leonard reaches his own conclusion about himself, and I can think of no better way to end this afternoon than with Leonard's own words:

"To answer the question 'Am I normal?' my answer is a provisional 'yes'. I am not perfect and nor do I want to be, but I'm satisfactory. I'm good enough. I have had a great life and I have enjoyed it. I'm just a bit weird"

Ingram Content Group UK Ltd.
Milton Keynes UK
UKHW020712260523
422386UK00010B/33